secrets

young
women
keep

Published in Nashville, Tennessee, by Thomas Nelson. Thomas Nelson is a trademark of Thomas Nelson, Inc.

Published in association with the literary agency of WordServe Literary Group, Ltd., 10152 S. Knoll Circle, Highlands Ranch, Colorado 80130.

Page design by Mandi Cofer.

Unless otherwise noted, Scripture quotations are taken from New Century Version®. © 2005 by Thomas Nelson, Inc. Used by permission. All rights reserved.

To keep the identity of those who participated anonymous, all the names and some of the details have been changed. In many cases, similar events occurred in several young women's lives and composites of the young women's stories have been used. Young women's stories used by permission.

Poetry used by permission.

ANRED: Anorexia Nervosa and Related Eating Disorders, Inc. http://www.anred.com, used by permission of ANRED.

Life Hurts, God Heals. Copyright © 2005 by Megan Hutchinson and Doug Fields. Published by Simply Youth Ministry, 26981 Vista Terrace, Lake Forest, CA 92630, www.simplyyouthministry.com. Used by permission. No unauthorized duplication permitted.

Thomas Nelson, Inc., titles may be purchased in bulk for educational, business, fund-raising, or sales promotional use. For information, please e-mail SpecialMarkets@ThomasNelson.com.

Library of Congress Cataloging-in-Publication Data

Hubbard, Jill.
    Secrets young women keep / by Jill Hubbard, with Ginny McCabe ; foreword by Stephen Arterburn.
      p. cm.
    ISBN 978-0-7852-2817-2 (pbk.)
    1. Teenage girls—Religious life. 2. Teenage girls—Psychology.
I. McCabe, Ginny. II. Title.
BV4551.3.H83 2008
248.8'33—dc22

                                        2008023086

Printed in the United States of America
4 5 6 7 8 9 RRD 12 11 10 09

Mfg. by RRD
Crawfordsville, Indiana
SEPTEMBER 2009
PPO # 98542

secrets

young
women
keep

by

Dr. Jill Hubbard

with Ginny McCabe

Foreword by
STEPHEN ARTERBURN

THOMAS NELSON
Since 1798

NASHVILLE   DALLAS   MEXICO CITY   RIO DE JANEIRO   BEIJING

acknowledgments

by Dr. Jill Hubbard

DEDICATED TO

my daughter **Noelle** and our friend **Marisa**,
two young women I delight in watching grow,

and to

Gene and **Kenette Molway**,
who ministered to me during my teen years and beyond.

A year ago this book was just an idea . . . and here we are! When Steve Arterburn asked me between radio calls on *New Life Live* to write a book about women and secrets, it was in a momentary pause before we were off to the next caller. Ideas began mounting, and soon the team of Arterburn, Hubbard, Word Serve Literary, and Thomas Nelson Publishers was rallied together. Not only were we all excited about this prospect for women, but a teen version for young women seemed a natural must-do. Thank you to all these men who felt I had a voice to reach women. And to the women's team who helped me actually make it happen. I am grateful to all who have played a role in the development of *Secrets Young Women Keep*.

My heartfelt gratitude goes out to all of the young women who eagerly contributed to this work. While most remain anonymous, their words speak out loud and clear. Through their stories and poems, their MySpace blogging, their national survey answers, and their sharing directly with us through personal contact or as part of the *New Life* radio audience, they have brought us to where teen women live and struggle most. Thank you for allowing us to learn from you.

To the young women I have counseled, from my early intern days working in adolescent treatment hospitals to individual clients through the years who have shared their secrets with me, thank you for helping me understand your hearts and struggles.

The teen years for young women can be some of the most turbulent in life, and I am grateful to be looking back having survived my own. During those years I experienced some of the greatest peaks and the lowest pits. Had it not been for God grabbing hold of me, putting key people in my life who could relate to those years, and pouring Christ's love and truth into my heart, I can guarantee I would not be writing this book today. I am grateful for those who taught me, supported me, and accepted me. Thanks to my youth pastor, Gene Molway, MDiv, and Kenette Molway, MA, my now friends and colleagues. Those who take time to connect with young people can have an incredible impact in the shaping of lives not fully formed. To the youth workers at Mariners Church in Newport Beach, California, who made church a fun place to belong and an alternative to worldly secrets—you made a difference and are symbolic for youth ministries across the years and nation.

Many thanks to my family and friends who have walked life's journey with me. And to those I have gathered subsequently at different stages. Thanks to Paula, Dana, Lisa, Jay, Dottie, and Mike who know the value and meaning of friendship. To my memory of Bill Winter, whose life was cut short but who had great impact on my tween and teen years. To my son Mack, who sat with me for hours, still not understanding how not to interrupt creative flow, but working on his own "books" while I worked on mine. To my daughter Noelle, who would listen to content, giving her own budding opinions. Amazingly, I have watched her transition into the onset of adolescence during the writing of this book. To Nancy A. Smith, PsyD, whose insight and wisdom I cherish.

Thank you to my agents at Word Serve. To Greg Johnson for helping pull the right people together. To Rachalle Gardner for her unwavering support and guidance through the daily tasks of writing and for keeping me focused on the bigger picture.

An extra special thank-you to Ginny McCabe for being my co-author and for having a heart for teens. For all her hard work, research, writing, and reworking; for hours of talking through ideas, organizing material, pulling together resources, being available day or night, and being willing to do whatever it took to reach the finish line. Your dedication and sweet spirit were a pleasure to work with.

Thanks to Marcus Brotherton for his creative editing and knack for teen-friendly verbiage. To the persevering Thomas Nelson Children's Books and Education team. It is an awesome task and a labor of love for all who invest in what it takes to bring a project to completion. I am greatly appreciative for all you have done to not just produce another book, but one with value and purpose.

Again, thanks to Steve, who pushes himself and others to be better and believes that if we can reach young people before their lives break down we are doing something worthwhile. And thank you to the *New Life* staff, volunteers, and supporters who are instrumental in the work of the ministry that keeps our show on the air, so that we can speak to hurting people who inspire us to write books that can hopefully help people live fuller, connected lives for Christ.

by Ginny McCabe

In writing this book, I would like to thank the Lord and my parents, close family, and friends for their unconditional love and continual support. I love you. I would also like to extend a special thank-you to everyone involved in the process of conceiving, writing, editing, and producing this book for making it possible. To all the young women who have shared their stories and secrets with us, I love and thank you. I appreciate your honesty and courage. I have had the opportunity to get to know each of you, and it's been a joy and an honor to be a part of your lives. I pray continually for each of you that God would show himself to you in real ways, and that you would be blessed tremendously and gain freedom by living a secret-free life. To everyone reading, I am also praying that same prayer for you.

contents

Why are secrets so popular?

by Stephen Arterburn

Co-author of *Every Young Woman's Battle*

*K*eeping secrets is nothing new. Way back in the Garden of Eden, Eve ate the forbidden fruit and didn't want to tell anyone. Adam ate it, too, and tried to hide from God. Secrets have been a part of human existence from that point forward.

Why are secrets so popular?

First, we think that secrets give us power over others. If we know something about someone else—or even ourselves—then we can control how people behave toward us ... and treat us.

Second, we think secrets keep others from having any power *over us*. If others don't know the real us, then we don't have to be responsible for our actions.

Dr. Jill Hubbard and I host a daily call-in radio show that reaches about a million listeners a week. For an hour every day, listeners (mostly women) call in and reveal their secrets: spiritual struggles, problems with friends and parents, food and shopping addictions, lust, struggles with drugs and alcohol, and more. People often call us in desperation. They are sick and tired of keeping their secrets. You see, when people hide the truths in their lives, those secrets have a way of making them feel miserable.

For instance, it's not wrong to want to be thin. But when a person wants to be thin so badly that she binges and purges, that becomes a problem.

Or it's not wrong to want to wear fashionable clothes. But when a person wants the right clothes so desperately that she steals to get them, that's a problem.

Keeping those types of secrets—and even secrets that appear to be "safe" secrets—typically always has devastating consequences.

I remember one woman who called in about a secret sex life she had while she was growing up. She thought it would not become a problem later on. But once she was married, the pattern of living a life of secrets was already well established. Soon that secret life resulted in an affair. The marriage she had always wanted was ruined. She wanted to know what to do. Really, the problem started when she was younger and learned to live with harmful secrets.

Callers like her are the reason why *Secrets Young Women Keep* is so important for you to read. The truth is, I don't want to hear from you in the future. I hope you never need to call in telling Dr. Jill and I that you nearly died, or you married the wrong man, or you're addicted to substances that now control you.

I care about you too much to ever want to hear your voice.

Secrets Young Women Keep dares to reveal some of the top secrets of today's young women. The authors funded a huge nationwide survey that told them the secrets young women keep.

In this book, the authors discuss the findings of that survey and show you how to lead an "open book" life. The key is how to live a life of genuine faith in Christ to help you keep strong when the temptation to hide knocks on your door.

My hope is that everyone who reads this book will gain the true freedom that comes when your life is lived openly, honestly, and with integrity.

Let's talk about secrets!

by Dr. Jill Hubbard

We all have secrets.
Big secrets.
Little secrets.
Silly secrets.
Serious secrets.

Some secrets are good: you don't always need to say out loud everything you think or feel.

But a lot of secrets can harm us. Secrets have a way of squeezing the truth out of life. Maybe we're embarrassed by our secret. Or it's so horrible we think we could never tell anyone the truth. Maybe our secret haunts us. It's always there as a reminder of something that's not the way it's supposed to be.

How about you? What's your secret? Have you ever wondered if others have the same secret you have?

A nationwide survey of Secrets Young Women Keep (we call it the SYWK Survey for short) posed this question: "What are some of the biggest secrets you keep?"

More than 1,600 of you took the challenge and responded. Topics ranged from eating disorders and cutting, to self-esteem, depression, pregnancy, abuse, addiction, and much more. You told us about your families and friends; how you feel about life, guys, school; how you sometimes feel down about how you look; how some of you had secrets in your past you felt you could never share.

We also met some of you on the MySpace page we created for you to discuss the topics most important in your life, and we appreciated your openness in sharing your stories both on the blogs and via e-mail. We merged the SYWK Survey results with the most discussed responses online, through e-mail, and in person to form the 25 chapters of this book. But in fact, you'll find more than 25 secrets in this book, because your e-mail responses were not always covered in the more formal survey's list of issues. For the two lists of secrets we worked with, see page xiv.

This is a book about real young women, just like you. In the pages to come, you'll meet a variety of young women as they share their personal stories. It's our hope that as you read the stories you'll get important insight on how you can better handle some of your own secrets.

We want you to be encouraged by how these young women gained hope and found a truer way of living without their secrets. We also want you to know that help doesn't stop with this book: it's okay to seek guidance from trusted friends, parents, or mentors who can help you when you need it most.

Undoubtedly, not all the top 25 secrets will specifically relate to what you're going through. That's okay. Maybe you'll keep one of these secrets later on in life (we hope not), but reading about it now will help you unlock that secret then. Or chances are good that you know someone keeping one of these secrets. Part of the reason to read this book is so you can help your friends walk through hard times.

Look for six special sections labeled **Stepping into a Secret-Free Life**. Within these pages we'll concentrate on the steps you can take to free yourself from a life of lies, no matter what your secret is. These sections will help you identify the secrets you keep, help you work through your secrets, then help shed light on understanding more about your most intimate feelings so your secrets aren't harmful to you anymore. And as you read and think about secrets, remember that Jesus Christ shows you a better, truer way to live. When your harmful secrets aren't there any more, your life opens up to the paths you were always meant to walk.

A brief word of caution: Throughout the book we give you opportunities to journal your thoughts and feelings. We encourage you to do that—writing things out can really help. But the caution is this: Books have a way of being passed around to friends, or left in the open where others may find and read them. These are *your* thoughts and feelings. That means they are yours and *yours only* to share. It's important that you get to choose if, when, and with whom you will share them. You may not always trust all the people who could get hold of your book. So treat your book like a diary or feelings journal, or get a separate notebook that you keep in a safe place and write your thoughts and feelings there until you decide to share them.

It is not our intention to "out" anyone's secret. Therefore to keep the identity of those who participated anonymous, all the names and some of the details have been changed. In many cases, similar events occurred in several girls' lives, and composites of the girls' stories have been used. Nevertheless, these are the real issues that are truly affecting young women like you today.

As you read *Secrets Young Women Keep*, it is my prayer that you'll uncover your secrets and be the real you. The God of the universe knows your secrets, and he loves you deeply regardless of what they are. His arms are open to you, ready to take away the hurt, pain, or embarrassment of your secrets. He wants you to be free to live the amazing life he calls you to live.

Walk with me now in the journey God has for you.

The Top Secrets Young Women Keep

Your Top Secrets

1. Family problems
2. Friends I hang out with
3. Hating the way I look
4. I don't exercise
5. Popularity at school
6. Depression
7. Music I listen to
8. Having sex
9. Smoking
*10. Alcohol use
*10. Drug use
11. Ignoring God
12. Debt/Spending habits
13. I don't like myself
14. Cutting
15. Cheating in school
16. Lost my virginity
17. Eating disorders
*18. Pregnancy
*18. Sexual abuse
19. Fake faith
*20. Pornography
*20. Suicidal thoughts
21. Piercing
22. Family heritage/race
23. Speeding ticket
24. Physical abuse
25. Tattoos

*tied on the survey.

More Secrets

Online and via letters, you asked that the following be included in this book:

- I desperately want to be loved.
- I have no idea what I want to do in life.
- I want to be the real me.
- I was raped.
- I have a hard time saying no to my friends.

WHAT SECRET ARE YOU HIDING?

*m*y friend Chloe had never been kissed.

One day she was riding her skateboard through her neighborhood and saw Brandon, a guy she knew from school. He was kind of cute, and she kind of liked him. And she wondered if maybe he liked her.

But that was it—for now.

Chloe stopped to talk, brushing her blonde hair behind her ear. Surprise! Quick as a wink—Brandon planted a wet one right on her lips! Chloe stammered and blushed. She had no idea what to do. Without thinking she did the first thing that came to mind. She closed her eyes and swung. She punched Brandon so hard his nose began to bleed.

Chloe skated home as fast as she could. The whole situation just felt weird. In her mind she replayed the events of the afternoon. Why had Brandon kissed her in the first place? And why did she react as she did? She felt stupid and embarrassed, like a little kid who throws a tantrum in a toy store. She hoped no one would ever find out.

It became a small secret, but Chloe resolved to keep it at all costs. Trouble was, a few hours later Brandon's mom phoned

Chloe's mom. *Why did that daughter of yours make my son's nose bleed?* Chloe could hear her angry voice over the phone. *Oh no!— The secret's out!*

Chloe's mom poured her a soda and they talked. The truth came to light. Yeah, she did want a guy to kiss her—some day, but the right guy, and probably not Brandon. She felt a bit taken advantage of by him. And true, maybe she had overreacted by punching him in the face. Maybe there were better ways of telling a guy to cool it.

IT BECAME A SMALL SECRET, BUT CHLOE RESOLVED TO KEEP IT AT ALL COSTS.

It felt better to talk about the incident rather than keep everything bottled up inside. Chloe's mom helped her figure out some things to say if kids found out at school. *It was no big deal, just a misunderstanding*—stuff like that.

Chloe also decided to write an e-mail to Brandon to apologize for punching him—he was a friend, after all. In the e-mail Chloe said she was sorry. But she also outlined some good boundaries of what Brandon—as a friend—was allowed (and not allowed) to do. Kissing was definitely out.

At least for the time being, Chloe thought.

While Chloe's situation resulted in what might seem like an insignificant secret, it illustrates how secrets happen. And although Chloe didn't realize it, she was learning ways to avoid the habit of secret keeping.

We've all got secrets—good ones and bad ones. Most of the secrets we'll be dealing with in this book are of a more serious nature—the kind that make our lives more difficult, those that have a way of controlling us, that bottle up fear and embarrassment. These secrets add to the stress and pressure we feel every day. If it's a big enough secret, it can actually destroy us.

How about in your life? What kinds of secrets do you have? What would you absolutely *never* want anybody to hear about you?

"Everything that is hidden will be shown, and everything that is secret will be made known. What you have said in the dark will be heard in the light, and what you have whispered in an inner room will be shouted from the housetops."—LUKE 12:2–3

What's the truth about secrets?

Not all secrets are bad. A good secret might be safeguarding a password on an e-mail account, or not revealing the inside scoop on a surprise party. The Bible tells us (Matthew 6:2–6) that we shouldn't be showy with our prayers or brag about what we do for other people. Those are secrets we need to keep just between God and us.

But some secrets definitely hurt us when we keep them. These secrets are in our lives because we feel embarrassed or ashamed, or maybe we feel that revealing them might cause us or others harm.

Those are the types of secrets we focus on in this book.

If you're a Christian, sometimes you might feel pressured to be perfect all the time: don't swear, don't smoke, don't listen to the wrong music, be happy all the time, go on mission trips, and be on the youth group leadership team.

So that's another reason we keep secrets: to cover up our faults. On the surface it makes sense—it's extremely *uncomfortable* for us to have our weaknesses, failings, or disappointments on parade for others to see.

But the truth is that everyone makes bad choices from time to time. Everyone sins and falls short of the glory of God (Romans 3:23). The good news is that as God works in our lives he transforms us into who we need to be. We don't have to walk around with our stomachs tied in knots, trying to be perfect all the time. We don't have to live secret-filled lives.

I'm not saying that everyone has to know our secrets. But sometimes when we mess up, we feel guilty about it and begin to plant the seed of a secret. As we water that guilt, the secret grows (sometimes sprouting more secrets). And the more it grows, the easier it is for the enemy to use our guilt to keep us feeling shameful, unworthy, and *not good enough.* Soon, we feel like we're living dark, lonely, and worthless lives. As long as we stay in the dark with our secrets, we allow the enemy to keep us mired in muck. And that keeps us from becoming who God wants us to be. That's the way Lauren felt.

Is there any worse feeling than getting dressed up just to be let down? Awhile ago this boy—who I really thought was cute—asked me out. I was so excited. I got all dressed up—you know, the perfect lip gloss, mascara, concealer, perfume, cute clothes, painted nails, straightened hair—and caught a ride to the coffee shop where we were supposed to meet. Time passed and he didn't show up. I just sat there staring at my cell phone, hoping and praying that it wasn't all just a big joke on me.

As I sat there, I thought about what I should do. Maybe I should text him and have the last word. At least I'd save my pride or get some response from him. I could say something like, "Hey, I think I'm going to hang out with my friends tonight; maybe another time." I felt so tempted to hate this boy. Or at the very least hold a grudge.

This is what I decided to do: Sitting in that booth, I vowed I would never tell anyone about this night. And I would never put myself in this position again. I would never be hurt like this again—ever.

I'm glad Lauren shared her secret here. But do you see the power her secret has had over her? It's true, she was genuinely hurt—but instead of talking out this issue with a trusted friend, she's vowed to hold her pain inside. Through her secret fear that this guy's behavior was a shameful statement about her, she's allowed her pain to enclose her and cut her off from all future opportunities. She believes she's protecting herself, but really her secret is keeping her from seeing herself as God sees her and living the life he wants her to live.

64% of you think it is **sometimes** okay to keep a secret. **11%** said it is **always** okay. **3%** said it is **never** okay to keep a secret.

Bringing our secrets out of the dark and into the light can allow us to gain perspective. When we identify and tell our secrets, we see that we're not alone. We understand that regardless of how "bad" the secret is, it doesn't have to define us. We are still loved and lovable. And we can continue to become the person God wants us to be.

Know your secret.

Some secrets come from everyday experiences, such as Lauren's, while others develop and become rooted over time. These secrets can become like monsters in your life, big stop signs that keep you from moving forward. But you always have a choice of whether to give the secret power over your life.

Right now, all I want you to do is identify the secret (or secrets) you have in your life. As surprising as it sounds, I don't want you to do anything about the secret just now. Revealing your secret is not always as straightforward as it sounds. Sometimes it's best to share thoughts and feelings, and other times it's best to keep the secret for a while longer. You have to know who you can trust, and when it's safe to share your secret.

We'll talk about who you share your secret with, and when to share, later in the book. But for now, just take some time and think about the secrets you have in your life. Write down those secrets that come to mind in the space that follows, either here or in a separate notebook. Maybe you will want to write a bit about how the secret came to be or how the secret formed over time. Or even how one secret snowballed into more secrets. Maybe you just want to write one word to help name your secret and bring it to light. You can list all your secrets or just name the secret that started them all. It's up to you, because this is to help you! So when you're ready, go ahead and name it (or them).

One step at a time.

This is the first step to living a secret-free life. Write down your thoughts in the space that follows or in your private notebook.

My secret(s) is (are)

_____

_____

_____

I hide my secret(s) because

_____

_____

_____

My secret(s) started because

_____

_____

_____

My prayer is

_____

_____

_____

_____

Amen.

My family is messed up.

We don't get to choose which harmful problems we'll face, but we do get to choose how we will react. Tara chose to keep a secret about her family, and eventually that secret ballooned into more secrets and she began harming herself.

THE SECRET

Tara's Story

Five days after my thirteenth birthday, my father walked out. He chose to leave while I was at school, so I never even had the chance to say goodbye. This loss left a huge void in my life, a void I couldn't figure out how to fill. Then, without my father's income, my mother and I had to move in with my grandparents. I felt embarrassed not to have a home of our own anymore. It seemed the harder I tried to trust in God, the worse my life seemed to get.

Like a lot of kids in this situation, I blamed myself for my father leaving. I was upset and angry. Rather than seeking help, I began to act out. In less than a year, I became bulimic. Then when I was about 15, I began experimenting with cutting. Soon the cutting replaced my bulimic activities.

That was several years ago now. With help, I chose to end my secret and talk about how I felt about things. I realized that I was not the reason my father left. I know now that God is always at work in my life, working for my good—I just didn't always notice the people he'd placed around me who were willing to help. I've stopped cutting myself and I'm not bulimic anymore. Now I see how God has placed an amazing calling on my life, even though I've been through some tough times, and for the first time I'm beginning to fully trust in him.

UNLOCKING THE SECRET

The absolute top response we received from the SYWK national survey on secrets was *Problems in the family.*

I know firsthand how hard it can be to have a family that looks and feels messed up. For many years I, too, lived in a single parent home. I know how easy it is for kids to blame themselves or feel pulled in two directions when their parents split up.

I also know that having your parents split isn't the only problem that families have in this category. Every family has its own share of challenges—some are more painful than others. *Problems in the family* can include a long list of issues. Maybe your parents fight a lot. Or maybe your mom is an alcoholic. Maybe your dad lost his job. Or maybe one of your parents suffers from depression or a chronic illness. Maybe you're in a blended family with half or step brothers and sisters. Maybe your family members are of different races or nationalities or don't speak English, and it's difficult for them to understand the cultural environment you face at school each day.

> *EVERY FAMILY HAS ITS OWN SHARE OF CHALLENGES— SOME ARE MORE PAINFUL THAN OTHERS.*

What's the pain level like in your family? Is this your secret? Perhaps you feel as Tara felt, that no one else would understand what you're going through. Or maybe you feel alone and unable to talk to anybody about this?

Here's the truth: No matter how strange you might think your secret is, someone will be able to empathize with your situation. You are never all alone. And although you might not be in control of the situation, you can be in control of your reaction. You might not be able to change your family, but you can change how you respond to the situation.

In Tara's case, she was angry, but she didn't know how to express her anger in an appropriate way. So she kept the anger buried deep inside, and the only way she allowed it to surface was through cutting.

Being able to express anger appropriately is important for a healthy lifestyle. That takes working through the problem with someone you trust, understanding your struggles, and learning to forgive the person(s) who had hurt you.

Ultimately, Tara learned to handle her anger in healthier ways, such as talking about the way she felt—which led to her ability to stop cutting. But there wasn't a magic solution. It took some time for her to learn to express her anger. And she wasn't able to forgive her father overnight. First, she had to learn it was okay to disagree with some of the choices he made. She had to see that she could still love him even though he wasn't all good and made many mistakes, and that loving and forgiving didn't mean she was okay with how he hurt her and her family. She learned what she could count on from her dad and what she couldn't, and how to speak up for herself more. God did not waste this situation in Tara's life, but used it to help her grow.

How hard is it to **talk** about your *feelings*?

Only **4%** of you said talking about feelings is easy.

I'd like to say there is a magic solution to your situation that will make everything better in your family within seconds, but there never is.

The solution is learning to tell your secrets: it's learning how to express your feelings, understand them, work through them, forgive, and move on.

NO MORE SECRETS

What's going on in your family right now? One way you can help the way you respond to things is to learn how to process what you're feeling. A good way to do that is to write a letter, because when you write out your feelings you learn to see what's truly going on inside your life. Your secrets aren't bottled up anymore.

So, write a letter to your family. Sometimes you might want to show them your letter. Sometimes you might simply want to show a trusted friend. At other times, you might not want to show anybody your letter—just write it and then rip it up into tiny pieces or use a shredder.

If your family is in pain, take a few minutes to answer the following questions, either here or in your notebook. You may want to use the following sentence-starters to help you begin writing.

Dear _____

Here are my observations about what's happening in our house:

_____

_____

When those things happen, here's how I feel:

_____

_____

_____

Instead of talking about how I feel, I usually do the following activity:

_____

_____

_____

I want to forgive you. With God's help I will. I might not be able to change what's happening in the house, but I can change how I respond to my feelings. The next time I feel that way, instead of doing anything harmful, I'm going to do something positive. [Some examples might be: go for a run, call a friend, listen to music, write down my thoughts, go outside, etc.] Here's what I'm going to do:

_____

_____

_____

Sincerely yours,

_____
(your name here)

Need help forgiving someone? *You may want to pray the following:*

"Lord, please help me to forgive _____. God, as you have forgiven me for my sins, I pray that I can forgive this person, too, over time. Heal my heart so that I do not hold on to any unforgivingness or hold a grudge against _____ and to know that my forgiveness doesn't mean I have to accept wrong actions. Help me to love _____ apart from his (or her) sin, just as you have loved me. Amen."

SECRET STRENGTH

"I have not hidden my sin as others do, secretly keeping my guilt to myself." —JOB 31:33

I hang out with people I shouldn't.

Your friends are a huge part of your life in your teen years. You spend time with them at school. You study and play sports with them. Maybe you just hang out at the mall or go to the movies together. The friends you spend time with influence your thoughts, decisions, goals, and even who you are and will become. That's why making wise choices is so important.

THE SECRET

Nicole's Story

Honestly, I have a lot of good friends, particularly now. But three years ago when I first started high school, I went through a time when I didn't know who my true friends were. It seemed like as freshmen we were all trying to figure out our place in school, you know—who to hang out with between classes, who to eat lunch with, what our place was, and so forth.

I was having a problem in youth group that year. I just didn't like what was happening there. But at school I met two girls named Mandy and Lindsay. Lindsay already had a reputation for being a bit "wild." But I thought Mandy was just a normal kid like me. At first, everything went well. Then one night they said they were going to a party and I needed to be there. Mom and Dad said no, so Mandy and Lindsay told me I should sneak out . . . and I did.

The party was pretty crazy. There were a lot of older kids there whom I didn't recognize. I had never been to anything like that before.

I had some beer. But it tasted funny so I didn't have more than one sip. Later we heard some senior guys were putting stuff into girls' drinks. I don't know if it was true or not, but that's what we heard.

28% of you said your **#2** secret is *friends you hang out with*.

Well, late that night I sneaked into my home through a window. I was feeling confident that my parents were in bed and I'd gotten away with it. Quietly, I went into my bedroom and turned on the light. Sitting in my room were my mom and dad. Boy, were they ever mad. We had a long talk that night. I was grounded for a long time.

Looking back on it now, it felt weird to sneak out, as if it just wasn't me doing it. Sneaking out wasn't something I'd normally do, and I wondered why I let Mandy and Lindsay talk me into it in the first place.

Mandy and Lindsay still sneak out and attend parties like the one I went to with them, but not me. We still see each other around school, and I try to say hi, but it's not as if we're close anymore. I know now it's important to choose your friends wisely.

UNLOCKING THE SECRET

Nicole made a very important statement: "It's important to choose your friends wisely." Good friendships can be very rewarding. But it's easy to be friends with people for the wrong reasons.

Sometimes you might hang out with a friend because you want to seem cool or popular. It's easy to ignore a person's character—who they really are—but we tend to become similar to the people we hang out with. We get into trouble when we give in to things we don't believe in because we're trying to look good to impress someone else. So take a good look at your friends and ask yourself the following specific, hard questions about each one.

- What sort of influence does this person have on me?
- When I'm around this friend, am I true to myself?
- When I'm around this friend, do I do what is right?
- When I'm around this friend, do I feel good or bad about myself?
- What kind of language does he or she use?
- Is he or she . . .
  - _____ a gossip?
  - _____ a flirt?
  - _____ overly sarcastic?
  - _____ angry all the time?
  - _____ constantly in trouble at school or home?
- Does this person use substances, such as drugs or alcohol, to try to be cool or to escape the pain in his or her life?
- Am I leading him or her, or is it the other way around? (Neither is a good thing!)

Friendships can be very tricky!

It can be easy to get caught up with the wrong crowd that can lead you to do things you shouldn't. Once that happens, it's easy to want to keep those friendships a secret from your parents—maybe even from other friends. Those are the secrets that can harm you. Deep down you feel uneasy about who you're hanging around with.

So why would you hang around with someone harmful to you?

Maybe God has called you to a special ministry where you're friends with the people who need God the most. Jesus Christ often hung out with all the wrong people—tax collectors, prostitutes, people who were socially considered "bad." But Jesus did that because he knew sick people need a doctor. He was leading them toward God. They weren't leading him away from God.

Or perhaps a childhood friend or longtime friend has started making bad choices such as asking you to help her cheat at school, or lie for her, or she's using drugs. Maybe you feel torn because of your history with her, your loyalty to her, or your fear of losing her as a friend. What do you do then? You could confide in an adult you trust to help intervene. You could try to guide her toward resources that can help her. But what if she's not interested in those options? What do you do then? As hard as it is, you might need to say goodbye to her—especially if she's making poor decisions and pressuring you to do the same. And if she values your friendship, saying goodbye might even be a wake-up call for her to seek help.

Saying goodbye to someone because they are making poor choices is very different from the social aggression and alienation girls sometimes use to pressure others to go along, conform, or to push them out. This type of peer pressure can start very early. One time I saw my daughter come home in tears from preschool because her best friend "uninvited" her to a birthday party. (I found out later the party never existed.)

In high school, this kind of social aggression among girls often gets harsher. Girls can be incredibly mean to one another, through the spreading of rumors, breaking trust by gossiping, and pitting friends against each other for the gaining of popularity and the avoidance of being the one shunned. Standing up against this kind of social/emotional control can be similar to jockeying for position in a swimming pool chicken fight game. In an instant you can be on top, voicing what others wished they could say, or crash to the bottom for saying and doing what others would never dare. Sadly, if you find yourself on the receiving end of that cruelty, it can be very painful. But the bottom line is that it's always better to do the right thing. Many friendships will come back around down the road. The girl who does what is right will be trusted in the long run by her friends. The girl who persuades everyone to do what is popular for the moment is seldom respected for long. If you or one of your friends is involved in something you think is wrong, dishonest, or harmful, you always have a choice of whether or not you will participate.

THE GIRL WHO DOES WHAT IS RIGHT WILL BE TRUSTED IN THE LONG RUN BY HER FRIENDS.

For example, Annie was an energetic and cute girl who always came bouncing into my office filled with animated stories of the latest drama amongst her high school friends. It was sometimes hard to keep up with who her friends were from week to week and who she was on the outs with. Even with things always changing, Annie would maintain that she could count on Shauna, her best friend since junior high. One week she didn't bring in her usual level of enthusiasm; instead, she was more sullen and went from tears to anger and back as she told me how Shauna was getting attention from one of the more popular junior boys and starting to hang out with his crowd—the ones, you know, who set the standard on who's in and who's out. Neither Annie nor Shauna had hooked up with guys as freshmen.

As sophomores, Annie and Shauna played on the girls' field hockey team, which practiced near their school's all-star guys' soccer team. They would watch the boys and talk about who was cool and cute and whom they liked and wished liked them. Now it was actually happening for Shauna. At first Annie had been happy for her friend, but then the realization hit her that Shauna was avoiding her when with her new popular friends. Sure, they still would talk on the phone after school and be at practice together, but Shauna was changing. She was dressing differently, more of the latest brand-name clothing, looking like a "cake face" in her attempts to make herself up like the older girls, and showing more skin. She was also, according to Annie, developing an edge of sarcasm and aloofness. Shauna told Annie that it might be better for them to spend time together away from school. Annie felt the pain of being left out by her friend, as if she were too young or not edgy enough to fit in with Shauna's new school friends. Actually she didn't like Shauna's new crowd. She would see them laugh or whisper and point out who needed their fashion help or better yet a makeover intervention. She would also see them snicker as she walked by looking toward Shauna, who would look the other way, hang on her boyfriend, and act like she didn't see Annie. In addition to Annie's feeling hurt, she also worried that her friend was being influenced in a way that could lead Shauna very wrong.

If like Annie your friends are making poor choices or if you have made poor choices of friends, you can ask God to help you stand strong, make positive choices, and build more rewarding friendships. Pray for your friends. Pray that you would build each other up, not tear each other down. Pray that God would bring the right people into your life and that you would be a good friend to others.

Sometimes God may call you to go through a season of solitude. When you decide to do the right thing, sometimes no one goes along with you. That's a hard place to be, but if all your friends are going in a harmful direction, it's always better to go your own way alone than to go along with them.

Although it may be hard to see the positive when you're in the thick of things, a season of solitude may turn out to be one of the most rewarding times in your life. Growth often happens in times of difficulty. Sometimes during those hard times you grow closest to God, or maybe you meet new friends you never dreamed of hanging out with before.

How do you find a great friend? Ask yourself, "What kind of friend do I want to be?" Develop those qualities in yourself. The qualities you like and appreciate about yourself are the same qualities you should look for in a good friend.

Best friends help keep each other in check. They look out for each other and always want the best for each other's lives.

How important to you are your friends? *Some of you said:*

"My friends are my inspiration to become the best person I can be and to reach my potential."—Bethany

"My friends are the ones who hear me out."—Nicole

"My friends are why I'm still here."—Liz

NO MORE SECRETS

If one of your secrets is the friends you hang out with, let's do some work in this area right now. Take a few minutes to answer the following questions, either here or in your private notebook.

Right now my closest friends are the following people:

_____

_____

Think about your friends. In each statement below, circle the answer that best applies.

1. I've lied to my parents about who I hang out with. *Yes/No*
2. I've wanted to be friends with someone just because I thought it would make me seem more popular. *Yes/No*
3. I've been ashamed or embarrassed of something my friends encouraged me to do. *Yes/No*
4. I've disagreed or stood up to one of my friends about something I strongly believed in. *Yes/No*
5. I feel like my friends are never "there for me" when I need them the most. *Yes/No*

If you answered "yes" to any of these questions, you need to think carefully about your criteria for friendship.

A good friend is someone who . . .
(Check any that apply.)

1. ____ is honest
2. ____ is caring
3. ____ is funny
4. ____ is compassionate (sympathetic)
5. ____ says bad things about others
6. ____ is dependable
7. ____ lets you borrow stuff
8. ____ takes more than she gives

9. ___ is patient
10. ___ has strong moral values
11. ___ dresses flirty and encourages me to do the same
12. ___ has a good relationship with the Lord
13. ___ sees the good in others
14. ___ is out for herself
15. ___ respects others' thoughts and feelings
16. ___ returns things she's borrowed promptly

(A good friend is not . . . numbers 5, 8, 11, and 14.)

Spend some time praying for your friends right now. You may want to use the following words to get you started.

> *God,*
> *Having good friends is so important to me. I know I've made some mistakes in this area in the past. Help me to have great friends. Help me to do what I need to do and be the person you want me to be. If I need to have different friends than right now, please show me what to do. Give me the strength I need to do what's right. Amen.*

SECRET STRENGTH

"Some friends may ruin you, but a real friend will be more loyal than a brother."—PROVERBS 18:24

I hate the way I look.

*a*s a teenager I was certainly not immune from worrying about how I looked. Each morning I tried on outfit after outfit until I got my clothes just right. I fussed in the mirror, hoping my reoccurring breakouts had magically vanished while I slept. I tried anything I could think of to cover up those zits. Makeup didn't work—it just drew more attention to them. Combing my hair more across my face helped hide them; well, maybe only a little. When I'd pass by a mirror, I'd look, always wondering if I looked okay or at least good enough.

Have you ever noticed how critical we can be of the way we look? I mean, when was the last time you walked by a mirror and said, "I absolutely love how I look and everything about my body!" Maybe I'm being a bit silly here, but I think it's easy for women not to feel content about the way we look, particularly when we're teens.

THE SECRET

Hannah's Story

For a long time I felt really different from everyone else. I couldn't stand something about the way I looked. Even now I don't feel comfortable telling

23

you what it is I don't like. I'd try to hide that part of my body, which was really hard in the summertime. So, especially in the summer, I spent most of my time in my room.

I know I missed out on a lot of the high school things, but at the time I felt like everyone would stare at this part of me and I would be embarrassed.

In one of my first college classes, I learned about something called Body Dysmorphic Disorder or BDD, a psychiatric disorder where a person has an extreme feeling that one of her or his body parts is ugly, deformed, or out of proportion to the rest of her or his body. And I thought, I think I have this. When that class was over, I started researching BDD and praying about what to do.

Today with God's help, I'm starting to see that God made me just the way I am for a reason. And I'm beginning to accept that the part of me I thought was so awful, really isn't. As my view of myself is changing, and I am less obsessed with my imperfections, I realize that no one even seems to notice what I spent so much time being anxious about. What a good and freeing surprise that has been.

16% of you **worry about your looks** more than **5** times a day. **23%** of you worry about your looks at least **once** a day.

Now I am using what I've learned for the benefit of others, helping them get through how they feel about themselves.

I wrote a poem about how the enemy wants us to feel, but how God really sees us. A portion of it that is almost like a daily prayer for me is:

> Oh, mirror, mirror on the wall,
> Can't ask who is the most beautiful
>   one of all.
> Please blind me from all my flaws
> That my confidence won't fall.

Body Dysmorphic Disorder, which includes muscle dysmorphic disorder, affects about 2% of people in the U.S. and strikes males and females equally—70% of the time before they reach age 18. Sufferers are excessively concerned about appearance, body shape, body size, weight, perceived lack of muscles, facial blemishes, and so forth. In some cases BDD can lead to steroid abuse, unnecessary plastic surgery, and even suicide. The good news: BDD is treatable by a mental health care provider.

—Anorexia Nervosa and Related Eating Disorders, Inc. (ANRED), (www.anred.com)

Unlike Hannah, who became obsessed about one portion of her body she didn't like, Emily's focus was on food and how it made her feel. Emily felt in control when she ate, but really the food was controlling her.

Emily's Story

I have issues with the way I look. Before junior high, I was confident in myself and thought I was normal. But after growing taller and developing earlier than my best friend, I began to think I was fat. In high school I went into a deep depression, and my comfort became food. I became heavier. Now that I've come out of the depression, I've started losing weight again, and I'm okay with the way I look.

I have to admit I'm still self-conscience about being heavier. The more I pray for God's strength, eat healthy, and exercise a little, I feel better emotionally and physically. My favorite physical parts are my eyes and my hair. Both are helping *me turn the focus away from my problem areas and toward my face. I'm still working on liking my body better. I hope my story helps someone else. God bless.*

 ## UNLOCKING THE SECRET

Hannah's and Emily's stories show the reality of how a lot of females think and feel. We are very critical of our bodies. If it's not "I'm too fat," it's "I'm too thin," or "I don't like the shape of my nose," or "I'm too tall," or too short. At certain ages it can seem like our bodies change overnight, and emotionally we may not always be ready for those changes, especially if it makes us feel different from our friends. We all want to fit in and be accepted, not to stand out as odd, unless we have chosen something unique for ourselves. Like sometimes we try to refocus the attention by getting piercings or tattoos—or maybe even going to a plastic surgeon. The list goes on and on.

If you've ever felt those self-critical feelings, you are not alone. Results from the Dove Self-Esteem Fund (DSEF) report that as many as 90 percent of all eating disorders are found in girls. In their teens, more than half of girls diet.

If we spent as much time thinking about our inner beauty and character and focusing on the qualities God wants to grow in us and less on all those darn flaws, we'd all shine as beauty queens.

Think about your own life for a moment. Do any of the following statements sound like something you deal with?

(In each statement, circle the answer that best applies.)

1. I'm basically a shy person. *Yes/No*
2. I have a hard time looking people in the eye. *Yes/No*
3. I feel self-conscious a lot of the time. *Yes/No*

4. I feel rejected a lot of the time. *Yes/No*
5. I fear failure. *Yes/No*
6. I complain about others quite a bit. *Yes/No*
7. I continually seek approval from others. *Yes/No*

Did you answer yes to any of the statements? Did you know that all of those statements are signs that you wish you were more confident? How you feel about yourself is often a direct result of what you believe when you look into the mirror. And mirrors seldom tell the truth!

Here's the good news: There is hope! God's Word is the true mirror. So start looking at yourself through his mirror. God created you. You are not a mistake; he loves you more than you can ever imagine.

Skin Deep

You look at me,
And what you see is what you think.
But that is only skin deep,
There's much more to me
Than what meets the eye.

God sees something different and unique.
He goes way beyond skin deep.
He loves me in spite of my flaws.
He knows the real beauty I possess.
He sees my heart, motives, and intentions
As my talent and character shine through.

Beauty is in the eye of the beholder.
You don't have to see it to believe the truth.

Love yourself and accept your imperfections,
Because what's skin deep will soon fade away.
What you'll be left with is what's real,
And the things that matter the most.
So, go beyond skin deep.
Skin deep is only skin deep.
—*Irene*

I love the line "Skin deep is only skin deep." Keep those words with you as you think about how lovely you are in God's eyes.

NO MORE SECRETS

If one of your secrets is that you don't like the way you look, let's do some work in that area right now. Take a few minutes to answer the following questions, either here or in your private notebook.

The physical feature (e.g., eyes, smile, hair, weight, etc.) that I like the most about myself is

_____

_____

_____

One thing I can do really well is

_____

_____

One personality characteristic I like about myself is

_____

_____

Describe how you believe God sees you.

_____

_____

Why is it important to see yourself more like God sees you?

_____

_____

My prayer is

_____

_____

_____

_____

Amen.

SECRET STRENGTH

"Charm can fool you, and beauty can trick you, but a woman who respects the LORD should be praised."
—*PROVERBS 31:30*

I feel lazy and fat like a couch potato.

i have to be honest with you: I hate to exercise. I hate the time and effort it takes. I hate the gym. I hate to sweat.

I love the feeling I get after having worked out. I love the ability to move and stretch. I love feeling healthy and knowing I've done something good for myself. Like Carissa, I've learned that the benefit of feeling good about what I put in my body and what I do with my body helps me overcome being a couch potato.

THE SECRET

Carissa's Story

You would think that after living through most of my adolescence and the cruelty of my childhood peers, that I would have done anything to make them stop laughing at me and saying hurtful things to me, and that I would have found a friend in exercise rather than in food—but I didn't.

You would think that after struggling throughout my junior high years with the need to be accepted and to fit in with the crowd, that I would have stopped eating to console myself and started exercising in order to fit into all of the coolest clothes—but I didn't.

You would think that after never being asked out on dates or to the dances during the first few years of high school, that rather than sitting in my room all alone listening to sad songs, watching sad movies, and dreaming of love, that I would have begun to hate food and love exercise—but I didn't.

You would think that after falling in love with the guy of my dreams—who was very athletic and liked walking and hiking and skiing and just about any sport—and listening to him plead with me to exercise with him and get in shape so I could do sports too—that I would have immediately gone to the mall, bought a pair of the latest gym shoes and workout clothes, joined a gym, started a diet, jogged and jogged, until I was a size four—but I . . . well, actually, I did this one—but it was short-lived.

When my boyfriend left me for someone more physically fit, I remember exactly what he said to me: "Remember so and so that we met at the retreat? She looked athletic and I would like to date her."

He broke my heart. I immediately started fasting and jogging to win him back. I did not eat anything, only drank water, and ended up running about twenty-six street blocks per day, and sometimes twice a day. I dropped the weight quickly, but I do not recommend this to anyone. By losing the weight, I thought that my boyfriend would come running back to me—but he didn't.

I gained the weight back, and my heart remained broken. A few months later, I asked my doctor what she recommended. She referred me to a nutritionist, who helped me work out a proper diet and exercise plan—and it's working for me.

My struggle with being overweight and not exercising has taught me something: Being the fat girl only hurts if I do not realize how much the God who made me loves me. Being the fat girl only leads to isolation if I don't know that God is with me everywhere I go, in everything I do, and is working everything out for my good as I love him and seek his plan for my life. And the same is true of you.

And while I still struggle with my weight and balance between eating and *exercising, I don't sit in my room alone crying anymore. I started by volunteering and working in my church, and that led to friends and working with other projects, and more friends, and getting out more and being happier and—yes—some dates. I haven't found the right guy for me yet, but now I think I will. And when I do, neither one of us might be running marathons—but we won't be couch potatoes either.*

So to all of you fat girls, skinny girls, tall girls, short girls—whatever your fear is, whatever your challenge is, whatever your sin is, whatever your weakness is, whatever your story is, whatever your secret is, the answer is the same—God made you beautiful. He knows your innermost being, all of your fears, wishes, hopes, and dreams, and he loves you more than anyone will ever love you. He has an amazing plan for your life. He has something great in store for those who seek him and call upon his name.

UNLOCKING THE SECRET

I *hate* exercising, and I *love* exercising too—how's that for sounding strange?

Maybe being a couch potato is your secret. It's not wrong to relax sometimes, such as a lazy Saturday afternoon where all you want to do is stay indoors and watch a DVD. But being a couch potato too much of the time is not a good thing. God designed us to move. He wants us to be healthy and lead active lives. That means getting off the couch.

If you struggle with your weight, I realize there might be more to what you're going through than being a couch potato. There are plenty of thin people out there who are just plain lazy, yet they stay thin. And there are some heavy people who are quite active, and yet they have difficulty losing weight. So the core issue here really isn't being a couch potato.

The core issue is deciding to live a healthy life whether you are the perfect weight for you, or too thin, or too heavy. It's deciding to eat healthy foods in moderate amounts, to attempt to live less at the all or nothing extremes and more toward balance in all that you do. There are no exercise police, and nothing bad will happen if you don't exercise for a certain length of time every day. That kind of self-imposed guilt is not good for you either. Learning to incorporate exercise as part of good self-care allows us to connect to and value the physical bodies God has given us. Here are some ideas for keeping healthy and making exercise a regular part of how you live:

IF YOU STRUGGLE WITH YOUR WEIGHT, I REALIZE THERE MIGHT BE MORE TO WHAT YOU'RE GOING THROUGH THAN BEING A COUCH POTATO.

- Walk and stretch and take stairs instead of elevators.
- Eat a small dish of ice cream, but not the whole carton.
- Eat carrots and peas and broccoli and cauliflower.
- Turn off the TV after an hour and go ride a mountain bike instead.
- Dance or learn karate or play basketball or kick a soccer ball around.
- Ride a skateboard or snowboard or swim or windsurf or skip rope or go to the park or run or jog or climb a tree or go for a hike.
- Do something—anything—other than just sit around feeling miserable.

It's easy to want to exercise for the wrong reasons. Being healthy doesn't mean that we have to run twenty-six blocks every day. In fact, that's probably a little extreme, if you're not used to it. Carissa admits that she is still working toward a healthy goal and that she hasn't fully achieved it yet. But at the same time, she recognizes that her value and true identity are not found through exercise or the number on the scale, but in Christ.

It's important to develop a healthy eating and exercise program that works best for you, one that will ultimately help you to glorify Christ with your body.

Sometimes I Fight

Sometimes I fight
To be the best that I can.
But there's always competition,
And I don't always win.

There's one place in my life
Where I never have to compete.
It's in the eyes of Jesus,
For His love makes me complete.

Some days I feel average.
Other days I barely measure up.
But every day with Jesus
I'm made perfect by His love.

All glory to the King
Who gives me power to overcome,
To daily rise above my ruins
And live for Him alone.
—Bridget

"I do worry about not exercising enough, but if I let myself, I can also become obsessed about it. I enjoy walking, playing soccer, and running. They are activities that bring me peace and can help me get rid of some anger. As I walk, it allows me to think and talk with God. Exercise is important. After I quit soccer, I gained weight and became lazy, but then when I started refereeing, I felt better about myself and lost weight again. I honestly don't put that much emphasis on it at this time. I'm getting things in order, and adding in one more thing might make my plate tip too far to one side." —Kelsey

NO MORE SECRETS

If one of your secrets is that you hate to exercise, let's do some work in that area right now. Take a few minutes to answer the following questions, either here or in your private notebook.

(In each statement below, circle the answer that best applies.)

1. I feel pressured to be skinny. *Yes/No*
2. My friends make me feel I'm overweight. *Yes/No*
3. I eat a lot of junk food in place of healthy, well-balanced meals. *Yes/No*
4. I look at other people's sizes and weights and constantly compare myself to them. *Yes/No*

If you answered "yes" to any of these questions, talk about your concerns over your weight and diet with someone you trust.

Read the following questions. Write the answers in the space provided or in your private notebook.

I want to be healthy because

_____

_____

One small thing I can do today to become healthier is to

_____

_____

My prayer is

_____

_____

_____

_____

Amen.

SECRET STRENGTH

"You should know that your body is a temple for the Holy Spirit who is in you. You have received the Holy Spirit from God. So you do not belong to yourselves."
—*1 CORINTHIANS 6:19*

I think I'm better than others.

Sometimes I receive letters that deeply affect me. Such is the case of Lacy, a high school student, who wrote to me about her secret and how changing her attitude enriched her life in ways she couldn't have imagined. Lacy's secret was that she felt superior to others, but what moved her to change is spellbinding both in its simplicity and in seeing God's hand. With Lacy's permission, I've included her letter here.

THE SECRET

Lacy's Story

The first day I met this eight-year-old named N'gouna, I wanted to kick him out of my car. That sounds mean, I know, but let me explain.

I got a part-time job working at a local charity. My job was to drive over to the housing projects and pick up a carload of refugee kids, then go back to the church, play games with them, do reading and math exercises with them, and help them with their homework. Honestly, I took this job because it paid well and didn't take up too much time. And I thought it would sound really cool to say, "I work with refugee kids." But it turned out to be more than I bargained for in many ways.

On my first day of driving to the projects, I realized I couldn't pronounce any of the four kids' names on my list. I knocked on the first door. The house was full of kids. Babies lay on the floor and toddlers stared up at me in wonder. Their pregnant mom sat on the couch. She couldn't speak English but spoke sternly to her two oldest girls, who went and gathered their backpacks and put on their shoes to go with me. I crossed the street to pick up N'gouna, a boy on my list. (I later learned that these two families who live across from each other share the same father.)

I felt relieved when I finally retrieved all four kids from three different apartments and got them into my car and buckled up. We all made it to the program. Each of us said our names, and we ate snacks. The kids were told to draw pictures of their summer. I was shocked when one little girl drew a stick figure with tears coming down her face. I asked her what the picture was, and she told me, "It was when this man hit me." I told my supervisor, and she said, "Oh, Latisha is always melancholy." Then we separated into groups and each group drew a banner. My kids fought because the boys were scribbling and the girls wanted to color nicely. The boys were yelling at me because they hated that their group's name was The Monkeys. But they were only pretending they were mad and then laughed out loud. When it was time to take them all home, we handed out candies for good behavior. N'gouna tried to take two, hiding one behind his back. But I took it away. He didn't eat the one he had, but instead put it in his pocket.

> I WAS SHOCKED WHEN ONE LITTLE GIRL DREW A STICK FIGURE WITH TEARS COMING DOWN HER FACE.

When I got the kids back into my car, I was tired, but I knew the end of the first day was near and I remained kind and calm. Then Abasi, who sat next to me in the front seat, began opening his window, unlocking the door, and taking things out of my glove compartment. Fadhila started to whine that she didn't get the candy she wanted and started pushing the seat in front of her with her feet. N'gouna unbuckled his seat belt and lunged at Abasi in the front seat. During that chaos, I was on the freeway trying to drive them home. I ended up taking the wrong exit and got completely lost.

That's when I lost it. I pulled over, pushed N'gouna back into his seat, and yelled at them all, "Get in your seats, buckle up, don't touch anything, and be quiet."

After I dropped them off, I drove in silence thinking, I don't know if I can keep this job. I thought I could be patient and Mother Theresa-like. I thought I would feel good about helping these poor kids, but I don't. I feel guilty that I'm not able to do more for them. They are annoying and their situation is depressing. Nothing I can do will help them. I can't take it. The boys are out of control. I can't stand Abasi and N'gouna.

I ended up keeping the job and got to know the kids better. After time I even looked forward to seeing them on Tuesdays and Thursdays, hearing the peculiar things they would say, and seeing their smiles.

On one of the last days I worked there, I was driving them home and it was time to give them candy. I broke up a chocolate crunch bar to give each of them a piece, and I noticed N'gouna was quietly staring out the window holding his candy in his lap. I was a little annoyed, thinking it was going to melt all over him and my car. I pressed him as to why he didn't eat it, and finally he said, "My little sister likes chocolate and I'm saving it for her."

I felt an unexpected pain in my heart. I stared at this boy and realized there was so much more going on in his heart and mind than I gave him credit for. He was trying so hard to be good. He thought about his little sister and wanted to make her happy. He probably worried about his mother who was always sick and felt embarrassed that his parents couldn't speak to his teachers. I realized I had grown to love this little boy.

I don't work at that job anymore, but I always think about those kids, especially N'gouna. He is so bright and kind and loud and funny. I wonder what will happen to him. I pray he is doing well. I miss all of them.

UNLOCKING THE SECRET

I've been in Lacy's shoes. When I was younger, I worked with Cambodian refugee children for a season. I often felt like Lacy then. I wanted to help people and do good, but I had all kinds of mixed feelings too. The people I was working with led such different lives from mine. They lived in small but very tidy quarters with large families and few belongings. Multiple children slept spoon-style across a mattress next to foul smells cooking on a one-pot stove. Some of the kids seemed so quiet, even in groups, I wondered how I could ever relate to them or what they thought or did for fun. Some had rotting teeth even though very young. In wanting to care, I needed to learn to value them first without thinking my help would better them.

When you meet people from different socioeconomic backgrounds, there's always a temptation not to understand them, even to look down on them, because maybe you're smarter, cleaner, richer, or perceive that you have a better family life than they do. Have you ever felt that way? Maybe you're keeping a secret right now about who you know or interact (or don't interact) with. Maybe you feel embarrassed or ashamed of them—or maybe you feel embarrassed or ashamed of your feelings or beliefs when you're around them.

One time a friend and I noticed a homeless man curled up in front of a drugstore sleeping on a cardboard box. People walked around him as if he weren't there. We felt sad and helpless. We didn't want to wake him. My friend put some money in the man's pocket, gently so as not to startle him. We didn't know what else to do. This man was unlovely in many people's eyes, but God invites us to love all people.

Prejudice, that feeling that you're better than someone else, can take a lot of forms. Maybe it shows up when you are around people different from you. Or when you see a homeless man on the street. Or maybe you are embarrassed of someone in your own family—a cousin, aunt, grandfather, or even a parent. Are you sarcastic to them or talk behind their back about them to others or secretly hope that no one knows you are related? Or maybe it comes when you see the unpopular kid walking toward you in the hallway at school. Have you ever laughed at an unpopular kid or remained silent when others laughed? Are you secretly glad it isn't you?

PREJUDICE, THAT FEELING THAT YOU'RE BETTER THAN SOMEONE ELSE, CAN TAKE A LOT OF FORMS.

The Bible has some strong words about this. God made each of us in his image. We all have a choice as to how we respond to God's Word. James 2:15–16 says, "A brother or sister in Christ might need clothes or food. If you say to that person, 'God be with you! I hope you stay warm and get plenty to eat,' but you do not give what that person needs, your words are worth nothing."

NO MORE SECRETS

If your secret is looking down on people, let's do some work in that area right now. Take a few minutes to answer the following questions, either here or in your private notebook.

(In each statement below, circle the answer that best applies.)

1. I worry about what people think about me. **Yes/No**
2. Sometimes I lie about who I know so I can appear more popular. **Yes/No**

3. I've done the wrong thing or acted poorly toward someone because I didn't want my friends to think less of me. **Yes/No**

4. I'm afraid that if I make friends with someone who is considered to be unlovely, uncool, or less than desirable, my friends will make fun of me. **Yes/No**

5. I've felt bad because of the way I've treated someone because of how they looked or dressed. **Yes/No**

If you answered any of these questions "yes," talk to someone you trust about how you can be more accepting of others.

Complete the sentence below.

When I see people who look or talk differently than I do, I tend to

_____

_____

My prayer is

> *God,*
> *I know you see all people as equal. Help me to see people as you do. Help me know what to say (or what not to say). Help me love all people equally.*
> *Amen.*

SECRET STRENGTH

"Love your neighbor as you love yourself." —MARK 12:31

WHY IT FEELS SO GOOD
(but hurts so bad) TO KEEP YOUR SECRET.

*t*he reason we keep secrets about ourselves is so others don't see our flaws. Why does this feel so good—at least at first? Because none of us wants to be judged by anyone else. If there's something imperfect about our lives—something we've done wrong, or something that's ugly, or something that we think that we'd never want known—we think that if we hide that part of our life, then everything will be okay. But it won't. So soon the secret begins to hurt us in many different ways.

"We should remove from our lives anything that would get in the way and the sin that so easily holds us back."—HEBREWS 12:1

Is your secret harmful?

Harmful secrets fall into two categories.

The first is when you keep a secret that involves some sort of sinful activity—either yours or someone else's. Maybe you cut yourself, or a friend has had an abortion. Maybe you can't stop looking at porn on the Internet, or maybe you can't stop eating and throwing up. You or someone you know is living a lie, but you're not telling anyone about it. You're just hoping you won't get caught or found out, or that your friend will be okay.

The second category is when you keep a secret about how you feel inside. You're not involved in a sinful activity, but you can't handle the chaos around you (or inside you), and so you feel one way but act another. Or you feel one way and *act out* in a harmful activity. In this category, you're not engaging fully in life. You're angry, lonely, discontented, or sad. And you don't tell anyone—you keep your feelings bottled up tight.

"I've kept many secrets. All of my friends keep secrets. I keep them because I'm afraid people will find out about the things I've done and the choices I've made. I'm afraid they won't look at me in the same way if they know—but I don't really have anyone to trust. Lately, I've started talking to God about my secrets, because he knows what I do and still loves me."—Rebekah

"I used to keep a lot of secrets. Finally I couldn't take it anymore and trusted a school counselor. He listened and helped me tell my parents. To my surprise, my parents already knew. They were trying to figure out a way to help me, but didn't know what to do. The counselor helped us all and got me into a group of other teens who had the same problem. I never knew there were kids with my problem. I found out later that my friends knew or suspected the problem all along. My secret really wasn't a secret. I don't know why we think we are doing such a good job at keeping secrets."—Erin

Why do secrets hurt so much?

When you go through life acting as one person on the outside, while you're really a different person on the inside, you can't have peace. You know something's not true in your life. It's like the band is on stage, but the guitar player is playing country-western while the singer is belting out hard rock. You cringe when you hear the noise.

It's also just plain tough to keep a secret for a long time. It takes an enormous amount of energy to live a lie. It drains you and robs you of the energy you could be using in countless other ways. When your life is a lie, you aren't living the way God created you to live. It makes your palms clammy, makes you sweat when it's cold outside, and puts an ache in your gut that just won't go away.

> "I keep secrets from my family, mostly my parents. My friends know some of my secrets, but not every one of them. I don't hide my scars from people I don't know, but I am careful to buy stuff at different places so the cashier won't know how many razors or pills I'm buying. Sometimes it's just easier to live a lie."—Aimee

It's easy to believe that as long as you keep your secret to yourself, you'll be fine. But the problem is that you spend months, even years, constantly keeping your secret under wraps, just hoping and praying that you won't be discovered. You can't stop thinking about your secret. It's becomes a part of you. And to keep your secret, you start having to lie or keep more secrets. You begin to feel like Aimee,

60% of you said you **sometimes** make **bad decisions**. **7%** said you **often** make **bad decisions**.

that living a lie is easier than sorting out the secret. But it's not. Soon, instead of being in control of your secret, it's in control of you.

When you refuse to share your feelings, you usually end up with two problems:

1. The original secret.
2. The problem you created by running away from your secret.

Often a secret takes root and grows, then it leads to other problems, then life continues to get more out of control as you try to get away from that thing that eats at you from the inside out.

The place to start . . .

To free yourself from harmful secrets, half the battle is realizing that you are not alone. When you're a teen, it's easy to think that no one else has the same problems you do. Maybe you think, *Nobody else is going through this, or no one else feels this as strongly and deeply as I do*, while all along, thousands of others are going through the same thing.

The problem builds if you compare your insides to other teens' outsides. You believe that other person's external appearance represents all of who she really is—when that's not the case. It's a vicious circle, really. You keep your failures and weaknesses to yourself so others don't see the real you. They, in turn, don't feel they can reveal their own secrets because it appears that everyone around them is perfect. Everyone is busy perfecting her façade, suffering alone, assuming she's the only one with this particular problem.

What you need to do is start talking. But here's where I want to caution you again. We're going to talk about who you can trust and when to share secrets in a later chapter, but as a hint

THE PROBLEM BUILDS IF YOU COMPARE YOUR INSIDES TO OTHER TEENS' OUTSIDES.

to that, just know for now that it is good to start out by sharing a little at a time. Remember also that when sharing your secrets, ask others for confidentiality and treat their secrets the same when they confide in you. Think of keeping others' confidences as a gift to them, treating them how you would like to be treated.

One step at a time.

In the first Stepping into a Secret-Free Life on page 7, you named your secret. Maybe you wrote a bit about how the secret came to be or how the secret formed over time. That's good. That was a great place to start.

The next step is simply to think about the ways that keeping that secret is harming (or will harm) your life. Maybe that sounds strange, unpleasant, definitely something you don't want to think about. But knowing how harmful a secret is can be a good step in being free from that secret. When you see how dangerous something is, you are that much more motivated to do something about it.

This may be one of the harder things to do, but take a few moments and think about the secret you named in the first section. How might this secret be causing you problems—either now or in the future? Maybe it's just added pressure in your life. Maybe it's threatening your life in some way, such as abuse, suicidal thoughts, or drug addiction. Maybe it's keeping you from being social or happy. Maybe it's something else.

This is the second step to living a secret-free life. Write down your thoughts in the space provided here or in your private notebook.

Keeping that secret harms me (or will probably harm me) these ways:

_____

_____

_____

_____

My prayer is

_____

_____

_____

_____

_____

Amen.

I just want to be popular.

*n*o matter what age we are, we all want to be liked. We want friends; we want someone to laugh with us; we want someone to trust with our secrets. There is not a time that this want to be popular runs deeper than in junior high and high school. Many of you wrote saying that you wanted to be more popular and what you were willing to do or not do to be popular. Following are the stories of three teens who have endured the relentless pressure of wanting to be popular in junior high and high school. See how each found her own identity in the process.

THE SECRET

Hailey's Story

When I was first in high school, I tried and tried but I never moved up the popularity scale. When I stopped worrying about it so much, I ended up having more friends. And they have been true friends I could trust. Friends who are always there for me.

My friends and I graduated together. Some of us started college this year; some decided to forego college for jobs—yet we remain good friends and keep in touch with online chat sessions, text messages, calls, and e-mails.

What I wish I had known when I started high school is that popularity isn't that important, and since I graduated it's rare I even hear anyone talking about who is popular and who is not.

Trisha's Story

I think popularity is overrated. I consider myself popular with the people who I hang out with at school, which is a rather small group of people. It's not like we are clones or anything, but we have each chosen not to use drugs and to remain pure (not have sex) until marriage—if that makes me a freak, then so be it.

> I THINK POPULARITY IS OVERRATED.

Marcia's Story

In high school I was just me. Everyone knew me, or about me, and I was never involved in a clique. There were the easy girls that went with the basketball players; the emo kids; the skater, art, and Anime fanatics; and the tech geeks, etc. Each group had their own MVPs and no group was greater than the other; they were just different. Anyone who bashed the other was considered judgmental and that was that.

I knew the pops in each group, but I never really hung out with one more than the other. I was able to connect with the majority of the groups to a certain degree, and I learned a lot from each group. I played sports one year, was involved in theater one year, joined a Christian club one year, and joined a Latino club one year. I was everywhere and it was fun.

I continue to be a social butterfly who loves all. I guess that made me popular in my own way.

UNLOCKING THE SECRET

When you're popular, "everybody loves you"—at least, that's the hope. The illusion of being popular is that you're cool, confident, sought after, adored. If this were true, who wouldn't want this kind of attention, but at what cost?

It's not wrong to want to be popular—as long as you're being true to who you are and what you know is right. The good kind of popularity comes when a person is genuinely confident and kind to others, and is liked for being a real person.

But there's another kind of popular that puts on airs, or looks down on others, or says other people can't be part of the group because they're not cool enough—that type of popular is hurtful, harmful, destructive. It comes from a place of insecure feelings about who they really are. Therefore, they must cover up fears about not being okay or good enough. They guard their position by making others feel small or bad about themselves.

> *THE GOOD KIND OF POPULARITY COMES WHEN A PERSON IS GENUINELY CONFIDENT AND KIND TO OTHERS, AND IS LIKED FOR BEING A REAL PERSON.*

It's also a problem when people go out of their way to be popular—particularly the wrong kind of popular. In those situations, a person will do anything to find approval in other people's eyes. A person will do or say things that really aren't true. Or a person will put on a façade, a front, where she acts a certain way but isn't really that way inside. If you find yourself doing things that aren't really you, simply because you want to be liked, then that's a problem. We all have room for improvement or blind spots about ourselves;

that's why growing is a lifelong journey. But getting others to like you means you have to start by liking you, by valuing the person God made you to be—flaws and all!

5 Tips to Popularity

1. Be friendly; smile and look in people's eyes.
2. Be self-confident and express yourself.
3. Show interest in others and affirm them.
4. Put others first out of kindness.
5. Always do what you know is true.

False popularity says just the opposite. In watching this kind of popularity it might seem like you must act cool, give half-hearted grins, look away a lot, avoid people's eyes, and don't show too much interest in anyone outside the popular group. You think you must be aloof and show others that you come first because you are special—after all you are popular and you don't want them to forget it. You must be outgoing with only the right people, or make others feel small and lucky to have your attention, or be kind only every so often to keep others insecure and maintain your position. Sound absurd? Is it? Ask yourself how you feel around the popular types; it may tell you a lot. Or if this is you, then how do you feel about yourself deep down?

The false type of popularity also carries a lot of expectations with it. To fit in, you've got to look, act, dress, and talk a certain way. Maybe someone says you've got to use drugs or have sex.

Those expectations can create a lot of pressure in anyone's life. When people are desperate to be popular, it's easy to overlook other more important areas of life such as grades, character, and a relationship with God. It is much more important to find favor in God's eyes, even though in a pressurized moment it can be easy to forget. It's good to remind yourself of God's desires for you when you're not on the spot and to make decisions ahead of time about how you want to respond when you find yourself in heated situations. Having a close friend or two with whom you can share ideas and support each other can really help you when you come face-to-face with popularity battles.

At the end of high school, I felt pressured to go to a certain college because the majority of popular kids I knew were going there. Even my closest friends could not understand why I wanted to go somewhere else. They thought I should go to a more elite school and that if I went to the college I was choosing I would not have as many career opportunities. The college I picked was a Christian college. People told me I'd miss out on the popular social clubs and parties. In their minds, I just flat out wouldn't be as cool.

BUT IF I HAD LISTENED TO ALL OF THE OTHER VOICES WHO WERE TELLING ME WHAT TO DO, I WOULD HAVE MISSED HEARING FROM GOD.

But if I had listened to all of the other voices who were telling me what to do, I would have missed hearing from God. In my search for a college, God was more concerned about the desires of my heart and his will for my life. As I made my choices, sometimes I needed to do what was unpopular with other people.

God had a much bigger plan for my life, and in his eyes my popularity didn't matter to him as much as it mattered to me. He knew my strengths and weaknesses, and he knew specifically how he wanted to use me in ways that glorify him. In hindsight, God has proven faithful. The college I went to turned out to be a great choice. I didn't miss out on any fun times. And my career has gone in amazing ways I never could have imagined. If I had taken the popularity route as my guide, things would have turned out differently.

NO MORE SECRETS

If your secret is wanting to be popular, let's do some work in that area right now. Take a few minutes to answer the following questions, either here or in your private notebook.

I think I (circle one) AM/AM NOT popular because

_____

_____

_____

_____

I think it's (circle one) IMPORTANT/NOT IMPORTANT to be popular because

_____

_____

_____

_____

The **truth about popularity** (three facts to help you keep perspective):

1. You don't always need to look cool.
2. You never need to do things you are not comfortable doing.
3. You never need to make others feel bad or look down on them to make yourself seem better than they are.

I think I (circle one) HELP/ DON'T HELP others feel valued because

_____

_____

_____

Some ways I can encourage people to be their best are

_____

_____

SECRET STRENGTH

"It is God's desire that by doing good you should stop foolish people from saying stupid things about you."
—*1 PETER 2:15*

I listen to music my parents absolutely hate

(and I think God would hate it too).

What type of music do you listen to? Many of you wrote that music can lift your spirits, make you want to sing, dance, have fun—and that's good. But others wrote about songs that promote violence, abuse, illicit sex, and other destructive acts and songs that make you angry or feel depressed—and that's not good.

THE SECRET

Jen's Story

Music has an immense power over me and changes my mood so easily. In fact, I am listening to a sad song right now, and it's making me feel down in the dumps. Sometimes when I listen to certain types of amped-up music I can feel angry or irritated. However, I try not to let myself listen to that sort of thing too much. I do not completely rule out listening to popular or secular music. I do selectively listen to some of it, but I carefully choose what I listen to. In fact, there are a few artists and songs that I choose not to listen to because of their lyrics, or because their messages are negative or destructive. What surprises me are the number of Christians who are not familiar with the wide array of great Christian music that is available today.

Brittany's Story

I listen to music that makes me feel happy, but I know my parents hate it. They're always coming into my room saying, "Turn that thing down!" Why do parents think everything is too loud? My parents are into really mellow old stuff; they like going to the symphony and listening to a whole concert without words. Sometimes it's okay, but most of the time it seems really boring. I know my family worries about me, especially since my older brother had problems when he was younger. His friends and taste in music had radically changed. His music became the more violent type with lots of bad language. He played it very loud when my parents weren't home. But after a visit from the police and a trip to rehab, he went back to being more eclectic and mainstream with not only his music but in most areas of his life.

Kylie's Story

Music serenades my soul. Anything that is popular or has ever been played on the radio is okay with me. Honestly, it depends on my mood. When I'm angry, I turn to rock. When I'm sad, soft emo music strikes me best. When I'm happy, I dance and go crazy to popular upbeats and lyrics. When I'm lonely, R&B drowns it and country helps me fight it. When I'm spiritual, worship music is best. During my silly moments, I call for disco, oldies, and old-school funk. When I'm cool, I throw on some positive hip-hop and rap. And when I'm sleepy, classical is best. Every genre soothes me in a practical way. Music is my life, and it gives me a way to express what's inside. I am currently not very content, so pop rock is guiding me past this season of my world.

. . . .

Praise the LORD!
Praise God in his Temple;
   praise him in his mighty heaven.
Praise him for his strength;
   praise him for his greatness.
Praise him with trumpet blasts;
   praise him with harps and lyres.
Praise him with tambourines and dancing;
   praise him with stringed instruments and flutes.
Praise him with loud cymbals;
   praise him with crashing cymbals.
Let everything that breathes praise the LORD.
Praise the LORD!
                                   —PSALM 150:1–6

. . . .

UNLOCKING THE SECRET

I attended a Christian music festival where all the hottest
bands played. It was such a powerful time. I walked away feeling
lifted up, refreshed, and closer to God. I wish that for your life as
well. You heard above how the girls said music reflects and affects
their moods. Music is wonderful because it can relax and soothe us
and help us get in touch with emotions that we have kept under
wraps. Music can break through our walls and can let down our
guards, but in doing so it can allow what's harmful into our hearts
as well.

Have you ever watched a movie that felt a bit disturbing,

where there was too much violence or arguing or something so tragic it stayed with you long after the movie was over? Afterward have you been aware of how you interacted with others? Were you ever easily irritated or found yourself picking a fight with a sibling, friend, or boyfriend? The media—what we hear and see—are powerful art forms. The point of art is to move us, to evoke feelings regardless of the direction that emotion takes. And if it takes us beyond our comfort zone, the artist has done his or her job.

Music is such an incredibly influential, powerful media. It can affect us in ways we never dreamed. Just think if the world were without music. Movies would definitely not be the same; long car rides even longer, and tuning out little brothers not as easy. Music is so woven into our lives that sometimes we're hardly aware of it or its impact on us, good or bad. A RAND Corporation study showed that more than 40 percent of today's popular songs contain references to sexual relationships and sexual behavior. The study found that the more time teens spend listening to music with sexual lyrics, the more likely teens are to have sex or engage in sexual activities.*

WHATEVER YOU CHOOSE TO LISTEN TO, PLAY, OR WATCH, IT IS IMPORTANT TO HONOR GOD WITH YOUR CHOICES.

"We are in a spiritual war, and we believe that the entertainment industry is providing the majority of ammunition aimed at our families," writes Al Menconi of Al Menconi Ministries.

Whatever you choose to listen to, play, or watch, it is important to honor God with your choices.

If you are looking for guidelines, options, or information about

---

* RAND Corporation study: "Exposure to Degrading Versus Non-Degrading Music Lyrics and Sexual Behavior among Youth," *Pediatrics*, August 2006, www.rand.org/news/press.06/08.07.html.

12% of you said one of your **top secrets** is the **music you listen to**.

how to make more positive choices when it comes to the music you listen to, Plugged In (www.pluggedinonline.com) and Al Menconi Ministries (www.almenconi.com) are two resources that address music, video games, and movies from a Christian perspective. For more help, check out the Resources section that starts on page 217.

NO MORE SECRETS

If your secret is the music you listen to, let's do some work in that area right now. Take a few minutes to answer the following questions, either here or in your private notebook.

Some of my favorite bands are

_____

_____

When I listen to music, it affects my
(Circle all of the choices that apply.)
Thoughts
Feelings
Attitudes
Actions
Behaviors

I (circle one) HAVE or HAVE NOT seen my choices in music influence me in negative ways (explain).

_____

_____

_____

_____

_____

Discernment is the ability to see things that are harmful or helpful, and then to make wise choices. Some ways I need to be discerning when it comes to music are

_____

_____

_____

_____

SECRET STRENGTH

"Brothers and sisters, think about the things that are good and worthy of praise. Think about the things that are true and honorable and right and pure and beautiful and respected."—PHILIPPIANS 4:8

Sometimes I feel really depressed.

*n*o one is immune to being depressed. But how do you know if you are in a depression or not? You don't. That's right, there are many levels of depression, and you could be clinically depressed and not know it. Sometimes a sad event or stress can trigger a long-term depression. If you are feeling down, talk with someone you trust about it today. Danielle felt sad for a long time, but neither Danielle nor her family recognized that she was clinically depressed.

THE SECRET

Danielle's Story

I was raised in a Christian home. I knew the stories in the Bible, and I knew about God. But religion never seemed all that meaningful to me. The Christian life seemed unrealistic and impossible to live out. I tried to follow the Bible, but God became someone whom I went to only when I had a problem.

The summer before my freshman year of high school, my mother remarried and I went from being an only child to being a middle child of four. Everyone was nice, and I liked my stepfather okay—but suddenly I didn't know where I stood in the family. Then my dog died. By the time I entered my freshman year of high school, I was depressed and anxious—and I couldn't break out of it. At school I acted as if I were happy and everything was okay, but on the inside I was miserable. Christians kept talking about how good life is when you have God, and all the joy and the peace that come with being a Christian. I couldn't stand them. I thought, Okay, I am a Christian, so why do I feel so miserable?

I cried out to God for help and asked him why he would allow me to feel the way I did. I was becoming angry and desperate and couldn't figure out why this was happening to me. I cried out to him, but continued to live my life in the same old ways. Around my senior year of high school, I came to the point where I was pretty much done with everything. I felt hopeless. If it weren't for God and my family, I might have ended it right there. I used to wish so badly that I could meet someone or something would happen in my life that would change it and take away all of my depression and hopelessness. I didn't really want to die, but I didn't want to live either, at least not the way I had been living. But I didn't feel like I could change it.

> *I FELT HOPELESS. IF IT WEREN'T FOR GOD AND MY FAMILY, I MIGHT HAVE ENDED IT RIGHT THERE.*

The summer after my senior year, I remember crying out to God again. I can't remember exactly what I said, but I know that I was at the end of my road and I was willing to do anything at that point to change my life.

One day not too long after that, I noticed that I had almost stopped cussing completely. I thought it was weird because I had cussed for so long and tried to quit the habit, but it always seemed impossible. Please don't think that I am saying if you cuss you are not a Christian; I am just telling you what happened in my own life.

I also started to notice that my perspective and outlook on life were changing. I had become very bitter and angry with God and the world, but I started feeling more sympathy and love toward others instead. When I realized *that I was completely hopeless and empty, I surrendered my life to Christ. He begin to change me and make me more like him. This may sound weird and crazy to some of you, but those who don't believe in Christ who know me would tell you that they saw a huge change in my life.*

I realized that the reason a real change never came all of those other times I had asked God for help was because I only wanted his temporary help until I could return to my selfish lifestyle, pleasing and living only for myself. After all, that's what life is all about, right? That kind of selfish thinking brought me nothing but discontentment. Nothing was ever good enough for me, and I was always miserable. I always thought I was a Christian because I had said the "prayer" and I was raised in a Christian home. But my lifestyle and my emotions never showed it. It was not about saying a prayer or living in a certain way. It was about surrendering 100 percent of my life to Christ, not 50 percent. It was about allowing him to change me, because I didn't have the power and strength to change myself.

UNLOCKING THE SECRET

Danielle was discouraged and suffered from depression, but God showed her how he changes people for the better. Depression can be a tricky secret. Everyone experiences changes in moods from day to day, but depression is more than the blues or the blahs. It's feeling down or just not your usual self for a long time. When that down mood (along with other symptoms) lasts for more than a couple of weeks, the condition might be *clinical depression*. Clinical depression can range from mild to severe and can be short-lived or go on for a year or more. At any level, it is a serious health problem that affects the total person.

Sometimes people think that if they or someone they know is depressed, it would be easy to recognize: the person would feel sad, hopeless, and would be crying all the time. It's true, if you are depressed you might feel those things. But did you know that if you are depressed you might feel agitated, nervous, angry, hostile, defensive, hyper, daring, restless, fearful, and/or worthless? You might withdraw from some (but maybe not all) friends and family, and lose interest in even your favorite activities—or you might start doing things that are completely out of character for you. You might find that your attitude has changed to a more negative outlook, that you are not caring about yourself as much, and that you even start doing things that are risky or get you in trouble. You might start sleeping or eating too much or not enough. You might have unexplained aches and pains, and it could be difficult to concentrate or make decisions. You might become tired or have thoughts of suicide.

OFTEN ONE OF THE FIRST SIGNS OF DEPRESSION IS NOTICING SOMETHING'S DIFFERENT.

Often one of the first signs of depression is noticing something's different. Sometimes you might be able to point back to a specific triggering event that started the downward cycle, such as your parents' divorce or a friend's death. You might feel unhappy on the inside but wear a smile around everyone, so it's tough to tell how you're really feeling inside.

Other times depression can appear like a nagging feeling or pain, one that doesn't seem to go away and then gets worse or more intense during difficult times.

If you think you or a friend is suffering from depression, there are things you can do to help. Depression is seldom beaten overnight. The first place to start the process is to reach out for help. It can sometimes be difficult to admit a problem exists. It can be hard to reach out when you are feeling bad. When depressed, part of helping yourself is doing the opposite of what you feel like doing, because you can't completely trust your feelings during those times. So talk to a trusted friend, adult, school counselor, mentor, or pastor. Asking for help is an important first step in freeing yourself from the secret of depression.

Danielle's story lets us know that there is hope and freedom in Christ, and that help is available. Christ is always at the center and core of any healing. Sometimes the specific solution to depression is found in talking things out. Sometimes medication may be needed for a while.

Feeling depressed? You're not alone.

Between 7 and 12 million American teens suffer from mental, behavioral, or developmental disorders at any given time.
—American Academy of Child Adolescent Psychiatry
(www.aacap.org)

NO MORE SECRETS

If your secret is that you feel down all the time, you may be clinically depressed. Depression can be a serious problem with devastating results.

As part of that process, take a few minutes to answer the following questions, either here or in your private notebook.

The emotions I tend to feel on a regular basis include

(Check all that apply to you.)

- ○ Loneliness
- ○ Anger
- ○ Sadness
- ○ Isolation
- ○ Hopelessness
- ○ Restlessness
- ○ Irritability
- ○ Worthlessness

Maybe you didn't check anything above. That's fine. You are probably not depressed. If you did check several of these emotions, you may be clinically depressed. If you suspect you are, can you point back to a specific time or place when you started feeling this way? The following sentence may help: I used to feel okay, but then

happened, and I started feeling down a lot of the time. Now I

One step I can take today in seeking help is to contact

There are many organizations that might be able to help you. Three of them follow:

- Depression and Bipolar Support Alliance, www.dbsalliance.org, (800) 826-3632.
- Mercy Ministries, www.mercyministries.org, (615) 831-6987
- New Life Ministries, www.newlife.com, (800) NEW-LIFE

For more organizations, check under the Resources section that starts on page 217.

SECRET STRENGTH

"God once said, 'Let the light shine out of the darkness!' This is the same God who made his light shine in our hearts by letting us know the glory of God that is in the face of Christ."—2 CORINTHIANS 4:6

I don't like myself and think others are better than I am.

*t*here are times when we don't like ourselves very much. Maybe we accidentally hurt a girlfriend's feelings or say something we regret. But if you feel you are worthless, not important enough to be treated with respect, like a failure, or for any reason consistently don't like yourself—you might have low self-esteem as Melissa did.

 ## THE SECRET

Melissa's Story

My life is a sob story of choosing to be with people who weren't kind to me, who criticized, yelled, hit, degraded me, and took away any form of dignity I had, which shattered my very existence and left me feeling broken.

To my boyfriend, I was an object, something nice to look at or perhaps someone to do something for him. I was subjected to verbal and physical abuse, and yet I craved his love so much that I stayed—with doglike devotion. I did not want to realize what was going on. I clung to small hopes every day.

With each one, I remember thinking, Maybe today he will hug me, or He doesn't know what he is doing, or He doesn't mean to hurt me. I blamed myself when he hurt me. I felt if I were better, prettier, nicer, smarter, he would like me and be happy. As he hit me, he'd say that something I did upset him; it was my fault. I believed him. If he said I was worthless, I believed him. And then he'd dump me, and say it was my fault—that I was unlovable—and I believed that too. And when he wanted to come back, I was pleased he wanted me.

But then he dumped me again, and I decided that all guys were incapable of love, compassion, kindness, and the ability to think of someone beside themselves. Then I met Dave, and he made it his goal in life to prove me wrong. I was sitting by myself in the far right corner of the room when he sat down next to me. He did not say a word. No cheap attempt at conversation, no pickup lines; he just let me work. When class was almost over and we needed to correct our tests, he turned to me and asked, "Can I borrow a pen?" That is what I needed for a person to enter into my life, a nonthreatening approach accompanied by showing no interest in me, other than as a classmate who might need an extra pen. For once I was not a fox to be chased. I was a person, I had value, and later he became my friend.

> FOR ONCE I WAS NOT A FOX TO BE CHASED. I WAS A PERSON, I HAD VALUE, AND LATER HE BECAME MY FRIEND.

It was not an easy task to become my friend. The idea of being alone in a room with a guy could give me a panic attack. The thought of having to speak to a guy could make me cry. We became lifesaving class partners. He was calm and relaxed, and I began to trust him. He treated me with respect and courtesy. He took the time to listen to me, understand me, and value me as a person. He helped me realize that I am worth something. And I began to like myself better.

With Dave's encouragement, I told my secret to a school counselor, who helped me learn a lot about myself and why I thought everyone was better than I am.

I still struggle with going out with guys, but I am not as afraid as I used to be—and so far I've chosen wisely and gone out with only really nice guys. And you know what? It's a lot more fun!

UNLOCKING THE SECRET

Not liking yourself is a broad topic, yet a lot of you said you felt that way. The topic scored high on the SYWK Survey.

Do you feel valued, loved, cared for, and liked by others and yourself? Do you have unrealistic expectations? Or has something bad happened that makes you feel bad about yourself? Have you been mistreated, yelled at, made fun of, or abused? The reasons a person gives for not liking herself are varied, but the end result can be low self-esteem.

So what can you do? A lot! First, remember that God gives everyone special skills and talents. If you're not sure what skills and talents you have, ask your school counselor if he or she has any skills tests you can take; talk to your parents and other trusted adults.

Start by realizing what you can change and what you can't change. For example, you can change your attitude, your outlook, how you approach others or present yourself, how you talk to yourself, your activities, your friends, your hair, the way you dress. Did you know that you tell people how to treat you by how you treat yourself? All the more reason to be kind and loving to yourself. You can also improve a skill through practice or learn something new. And you can certainly change your mind about something or make a new choice.

There are really lots of things you can change about you and your life when you think about it. So why is it that we give so much energy to the things we can't change? We are so afraid that our faults and flaws are as glaring to others as they are to us. But the truth is they just aren't, and that's a good secret to know. Then we have to grieve that we are not perfect and learn to lovingly live with the things we can't change. For instance, we can't change past poor choices and may have to live with the consequences, but we can always express regret and make a choice to right our wrongs as much as possible. We also can't change how short or tall we are, our body type, our general personality, our family, our ethnicity, where our parents choose to live, or whether they stay married or divorce, and—while we might have some influence—ultimately, we can't change other people. We also can't change the heart of God. We can make him sad by some of our choices, but we can never change his love for us—and that is a good thing to not be able to change!

Other things you can change . . .

- When you meet someone, smile, stand tall, look that person in the eye, and say hello.
- When you have a negative thought like *I'm really bad at tennis!*— counter it with two positive thoughts like, *I'm smart. I'll practice more and do better next time.*
- Focus more on what you are good at.
- Try to minimize comparing yourself to others.
- Be prepared for your day.
- Forgive yourself.
- Don't be afraid to try something new or different.
- Set realistic goals.
- Compliment yourself.
- Accept compliments from others graciously and write them down to reflect back on.

Something else you can do is think about what you'd do if you could do anything in the world. Where would you go, how would you look, who would you take with you? Now consider doing something toward that goal. Maybe your dream is to be a counselor or help others learn new skills or develop a new computer program or video game. Whatever it is you'd like to do, ask your parents (or another trusted adult) to help you develop a plan toward your dream goal. And you know what? If in the middle of your plan you decide you'd rather be a painter than a surfer—it's okay because this is all about you, having fun, and discovering your skills.

In your plan include something small you can do every day that makes you feel good about yourself. It might be reading a chapter in a book, going for a walk, listening to a friend, doing your nails, watching a movie, making a special meal. Maybe it's taking time to play with the family pets or volunteering at your church or planting something and watching it grow. Maybe it's a brand-new look! It's up to you. Keep a journal of the things that you do that make you feel good about yourself—and give yourself a point for each one.

ULTIMATELY, A PERSON'S CONFIDENCE MUST BE IN CHRIST.

Your invitation is to explore your options, take responsibility for your part in helping the healing process, and reach out for the right kind of help. Some of those options are in the Resources section that starts on page 217.

Ultimately, a person's confidence must be in Christ. If you have been let down or have felt unsafe in your past, it means you may need to work toward developing trust again and rebuilding confidence. God sees all of your tears and cries with you. God has not called you to have a spirit of fear but of hope (1 John 4:9–18).

Like No Other Love
Never before
Has there been a love
Like yours
It's like no other

Like colored leaves in autumn
Like the smell of the air in spring
Like pure white snow in winter
Like basking in summer's heat

Your love has the power
To not just save my soul
But your love has the power
To come and make me whole

Yours is a love
That comes from on high
Yours is a love
That is willing to die

Yours is a love
Pure and timely
Yours is a love
Immeasurable and mighty

Come down from Heaven
Poured out like a drink
To a dry and thirsty soul
Your love came to me

Never before
Has there been a love
Like yours
It's like no other
—Janna

NO MORE SECRETS

If your secret is that you don't like yourself, let's take some time right now to do some work in this area. Take a few minutes to answer the following questions, either here or in your private notebook.

The places where I feel encouraged in my life are

(Check all that apply.)

- ◯ Home
- ◯ School
- ◯ Work
- ◯ Church
- ◯ Youth group
- ◯ Hanging out with friends
- ◯ Friend's house
- ◯ Grandparent's home
- ◯ Someplace else

What do you typically do when you receive negative feedback?

_____

_____

_____

When bad things happen, are you able to tell others or do you see most things as your fault? Why?

_____

_____

_____

_____

Who in your life makes you feel encouraged?

_____

_____

_____

Write a list of positive thoughts and post them somewhere you see them every day. Your list could include things like . . .

- Today will be a good day for me.
- I'm smart.
- God is with me.
- God believes in me.
- God made me exactly the way he wanted me to be.

_____

_____

_____

Every day write down something that made you happy.

_____

_____

_____

My dream goal is to _____ .

I can do that by

_____

_____

_____

My prayer is

> *God,*
> *Please help me to put my trust in you and help me to overcome my negative feelings about myself and to see myself more like you see me. Allow me to face my situation with confidence and to seek help when it is necessary. God, continue to protect my heart and my thoughts from evil, bring the right kind of people into my life, and help me to see your will for me in every situation.*
> *Amen.*

SECRET STRENGTH

"I can do all things through Christ, because he gives me strength."—PHILIPPIANS 4:13

I ignore God.

god has as many ways to come into our lives as there are blades of grass in the universe. He might choose to get our attention in an obvious way or to be more subtle and allow us to discover him in a surprising way, as he did with Jessica and Mickayla.

THE SECRET

Jessica's Story

I was almost 16 and watching a late-night cable show that I really wasn't supposed to watch. The show had a lot of sex in it, and I was watching the door to the study to be sure my parents didn't wake up and walk in on me. It wasn't the first time I'd watched these shows, but this time the characters started saying derogatory things about God.

> **I WAS PLAYING GAMES WITH THE DEVIL, BUT I HAD HAD ENOUGH.**

To my surprise, I burst into tears. I realized that I had been giving into temptation by allowing myself to be obsessed with this secret and using it for wrong purposes. I realized that I had been ignoring God's Word, doing what I wanted to do, and pretending that it was okay. I'd convinced myself that I wasn't really doing anything that harmful.

I was playing games with the devil, but I had had enough. God wanted to win the game and he did. I accepted Christ into my life, and now I choose to do his will. I pray that every day he will guide me and use me to shine his light.

The Scripture verse I say every day to remind me to keep God in my life is 1 John 1:9: "But if we confess our sins, he will forgive our sins, because we can trust God to do what is right. He will cleanse us from all the wrongs we have done."

Mickayla's Story

When I was 15, it was easy for me to ignore God. My family had moved across country, and my parents were so busy that they hadn't taken time to find a church for us. And I decided I'd like to be someone different from the "quiet" girl from my last school. I wanted to be someone wild and adventurous. Popular. And I didn't see how God fit in new my life. After all, how adventurous could a Christian be?

So I joined this group that took outdoor adventures. I was nervous thinking about all the new activities we were going to do like rappelling and white-water rafting.

It turned out the leader was well-known as an outdoorsman. He must have noticed I was nervous, because he came over to talk to me. He said that what he did was to trust God. I was startled. Later we had a long talk about being a Christian, and I realized I could be adventurous and liked, and be a Christian too.

UNLOCKING THE SECRET

How many of us have sin locked in our closets? How many times has God reminded us to confess? He said he would give us a clean slate by offering us forgiveness. At times, we all do things that do not please God, but he asks us to seek him and do what is right. It might seem like it is much easier to ignore or hide what we've done wrong, because if we face it, we might have to change our actions, our behavior, and the consequences may seem too great.

God reaches out to us in surprising ways. He got Jessica's attention through a late-night x-rated TV show to help her realize her own wrongful secrets and to confess her sins to him. For Mickayla it was an outdoor adventure. God calls each of us to confess our sins to him so we can be freed from our mistakes.

There are so many things around us that tempt us and try to bring us down. Maybe you are currently involved in some kind of activity or heart attitude that you know God is not pleased with. But if you seek him, he can change your heart.

Sometimes we ignore God because we think we know it all or we have all the answers, but we don't. We tend to forget about Christ and to get caught up in our own agendas. Even when we lose sight of God, he is always there for us.

Once I had a misunderstanding with a friend. We both needed to apologize and say we were sorry before we could forgive each other for the wrong that had been done. It would have been much easier not to face one another or talk about it. But once we broke the ice, relief followed, and we were able to work out the misunderstanding. In the end, this small act of forgiveness strengthened our friendship.

Our relationship with God is similar to our human relationships. We need to be honest and open with him, and share what's on our hearts. Sometimes that can be difficult. We all have impure thoughts, deeds, and actions, but there is freedom in confessing our sins to God and to one another, and asking God to make everything right again.

NO MORE SECRETS

If your secret is ignoring God, let's do some work in this area right now. Take a few minutes to answer the following questions, either here or in your private notebook.

Has there ever been a time in your life when you felt like you were ignoring God? If so, when and why?

_____

_____

_____

_____

Do you ever think it is easier to ignore God rather than face him? Why or why not?

_____

_____

_____

_____

What has God done to get your attention?

_____

_____

_____

Why is it sometimes hard for you to be open and honest with God?

_____

_____

_____

_____

Write about a time you felt better after confessing your sins to God.

_____

_____

_____

_____

Following are some ways that can help you focus on God:

(Check the ones you've done or will do today.)

____ Read the Bible and learn about what God has to say to you.

____ Pray and talk to God about what is going on in your life.

____ Share God with your friends by talking about him.

____ Do what God asks by obeying his Word.

____ Serve God by getting involved in a ministry at your church.

____ Help a friend who is in need.

SECRET STRENGTH

"Jesus answered, 'I tell you the truth, everyone who lives in sin is a slave to sin.'" — JOHN 8:34

YOU CAN'T TRUST EVERYONE, BUT YOU CAN TRUST SOMEONE.

So, what do you do with your secret? How do you get your secret to stop being a burden?

Simple: You tell it!

When you tell it, the pressure lifts. Often you have a new understanding of a new direction to take. You're on your way to a truer, more authentic way of living.

But here's where things get a bit tricky, because you don't want to tell your secret(s) to just anyone or to everyone. So who do you share your secret(s) with, and how do you go about moving from the darkness of living a lie to the light of a secret-free life?

"But the people who trust the LORD will become strong again. They will rise up as an eagle in the sky; they will run and not need rest; they will walk and not become tired."—ISAIAH 40:31

Thinking it through . . .

It seems simple: When you decide to share your secret, give your-self (or each other—if the secret is your friend's) the time to prepare yourself to open up and share.

In a perfect world, secrets are best shared when you're ready and the time is right. After you've had time to reflect on it and decide who is a safe person who will care about your feelings and be willing to listen, pick a time when everyone is available and free from distractions. But we don't live in a perfect world. If you're in the middle of a traumatic situation—such as someone in your fam-ily being ill—you might be in survival mode. That means your first task may be just to get through the other side of the trauma before you can deal with the feelings or before you share your secret. However, we often need others in the midst of a crisis or traumatic situation so we don't have to go it alone. There are no awards for handling life's difficulties by yourself. And if your secret is contrib-uting to the trauma—such as being pregnant, hurting yourself, using drugs, acting out—you'll need to find someone to trust . . . and fast. (The same is true if it is a friend who is in the middle of a traumatic situation. If your friend is talking about ending her life because her boyfriend broke up with her—don't wait; take it seriously.)

Even if you don't have a secret right now, it's a good idea to think about adults you'd trust with your secret or a friend's secret. Having a mental list of trusted, supportive people in your life is important to consider before the crisis or problem hits. Knowing who you would go to means you have taken the time to think about resources or, better yet, that you have developed some con-nections with adults and friends. Those connections can make all the difference in the outcome of a situation or how you feel about it and yourself in the process. Sharing your secret about a wrong choice can keep you from months or even years of shame about yourself; it can stop you from continuing down a path you know is wrong.

Is it ever okay to break a trust and tell someone's secret?

You should respect a person who tells you a secret by keeping her confidence safe and by keeping the secret to yourself. Most secrets that are told to us by a friend are not ours to share. Consider it an honor to be trusted and be a safe person for her, just as you would want her to be for you. *However, there are a few exceptions to that rule.* If a friend tells you a secret that could bring harm to herself or someone else, then you *must* tell an appropriate person who will be able to help her. For example, if a friend tells you in secret that she is thinking suicidal thoughts, or that a family member is sneaking into her room at night and touching her, you must tell someone because these are life-impairing situations. The same is true if she tells you she's thinking about hurting someone else.

By telling you her secret, your friend is reaching out for help—whether she realizes it or not. It's important that you do not try to counsel her yourself. Professionals study for many years to learn how to reach people who are considering hurting themselves or others or dealing with abuse. She might even need medication or hospitalization. She might need long-term treatment. So if a friend tells you she might harm herself or others, or someone is harming her, you should seek help for her immediately. You might start by letting her know that her situation may be bigger than the two of you can handle. Encourage her to go to an adult who could help, and tell her you will go with her. If she refuses, suggest you both tell another friend who can help support her. Try to make sure she is with others and not alone, and then you should seek out an adult who could intervene. Better to have your friend mad at you than have her make a permanent, irreversible decision. Often friends will tell you to keep their dangerous secret, but it is better to go to a trusted adult in your life who can help you weigh out whether to tell or not to tell. Some secrets of others can become your secrets when the burden is too big for you to bear, and seeking wise counsel is how you can help yourself and your friend.

BY TELLING YOU HER SECRET, YOUR FRIEND IS REACHING OUT FOR HELP— WHETHER SHE REALIZES IT OR NOT.

So in cases like these, who should you tell? If you believe your friend's life or the lives of others could be or is in immediate danger, call 9-1-1. Otherwise, quickly seek out a parent, a teacher, a school counselor, a youth minister, or a pastor for guidance in determining what steps to take.

Which friends do you trust?

When you have a secret, the key is not to tell that secret to everyone you meet. Who you bring into your confidence depends on the nature of what you're holding inside.

Usually, you'll trust someone you've known a long time more

than a new friend. But what if you've moved or for some other reason you are no longer in touch with your best friends? Then you might be tempted to trust a new friend.

Whenever you make a new friend, initially there's a feeling like you want to tell her all about yourself right away—and she probably feels the same way. But deeper friendships are formed over time. Trust is developed as you get to know that person and she gets to know you. Resist the impulse to tell a new friend everything about yourself right at once. Make sure that person is trustworthy. A good rule of thumb before you share anything personal about yourself is to ask the question: "How long have I known this person?" If it's only a short time, consider sharing only a small secret or a little of your secret.

Occasionally things get shared with the wrong people. You take a risk hoping to develop a closer relationship with someone. But sharing too much with the wrong people leaves us vulnerable. It's okay not to share everything with everybody. If you are wondering who to share your secret with, it's okay to be cautious early on in a relationship. In developing friendships, it is always better to share little bits of information gradually rather than all at once; this helps trust to grow. Never share your biggest secret first, though it might feel good at the moment.

38% of you said that **parents/ guardians** have the biggest influence on **how you feel about yourselves**. **33%** said the next biggest influence is **your friends**.

Sometimes you might share a secret and the other person doesn't believe you. It might be because the person is in denial or is not paying close attention or is working through his or her own problems. Don't despair. Go to someone else on your list, or to a resource (such as those in the Resources section starting on page 217) or to someone else on your Action Plan (see page 214).

Telling secrets to your parents.

I am a parent, so I can tell you that most parents want their children to come to them with anything and everything. It's a good parent's responsibility to create an environment where a child feels comfortable to do that.

If you can talk easily with your parents and share things, and if they've demonstrated a history of not freaking out when you tell them things, that's great! But if you a feel like you are unable to talk to your parents, or if you have a hard time getting their attention or knowing if they are interested in what you have to say, start by asking them a question or two. It might be something as simple as, "How was your day, Mom?" or "Dad, how do you feel about whatever?" You might also start by asking them about what it was like for them when they were your age, or if they talked very much to their parents. You might be surprised by what you hear.

Begin to share secrets with your parents by sharing smaller things with them, or talking about the idea of talking before you tell them your secrets. My daughter gave me permission to share her technique for starting conversations with me: She says, "Mom, I feel like talking to you, but I'm not sure what I want to talk about."

She is letting me know that she wants to connect and needs some attention from me. She is testing the waters to see if I am emotionally available to hear her. (Of course, it can also be because she is trying to avoid bedtime.) But in talking about talking we open up the space for more meaningful sharing and trust.

If you decide to share your secret with your parents and feel nervous or uneasy about it, ask yourself, "What's the worst that can happen?" Imagine that scenario—it might help to ease the pressure you're feeling. In many instances, once you get past your parents' initial reaction, you will be able to work through challenges or problems together. Tell them what you need from them. For example, say: "Mom, I need you to listen to some things that are hard for me to say, and it would help if you could respond only when I am finished—okay?" or "Dad, I just need to bounce some ideas off of you. Can you listen for a few minutes?"

You might be afraid to share with your parents because you think that they will be disappointed in you. That's a normal fear. But take the chance. Remember, life is not about being perfect. It's about being the true you without the camouflage of lies.

If your parents freak out when you tell them your secret, try to relax and give them time to sort things out in their own minds. Remember, you know the secret and set the time and place to talk. This is brand-new to your parents, and they have emotions too. No parent is able to meet your needs perfectly or respond perfectly all the time. Share your secret with them anyway.

Keep in mind that not all parents are equal. If you have a genuinely abusive parent, or a parent who denies her or his own problems, or who hasn't or doesn't believe you, it is only natural that you do not want to tell her or him your secrets because you do not feel emotionally or physically safe. If by telling your secret to your parent you are convinced that more harm would come to you, then find another trusted adult to tell your secret to first.

When you can't tell your parents, tell someone!

No matter what, it is important for you to have a trusted adult you can talk to and confide in. The ideal choice is your parents. But if you feel like you can't talk to your parents, seek out a teacher, school counselor, youth minister, pastor, parent of a friend, another family member such as your aunt or grandma, or family friend. An older person can offer advice and perspective that a younger person is typically not going to be able to offer.

One step at a time.
This is the third step to living a secret-free life. Write down your thoughts in the space here or in your private notebook.

The people my own age I'm closest to right now are

_____

_____

_____

The adults I trust the most right now are

_____

_____

My prayer is

Lord Jesus,
Please help me know who to trust, and the best time and way
to tell my secret. I pray right now for the person whom I tell my
secret to that she (or he) would be able to listen with wisdom,
and point me in the way of understanding. And help me to listen
to what the person says—even if it is not what I want to hear. I
want to be secret-free.
Amen.

I have money problems—my spending is out of control.

So what do you do with your money? Do you save it or spend it immediately? Do you depend on the generosity of your parents or have an after-school job? Do you put any money aside for college, a car, or that apartment you want sometime soon? And what do you spend your money on? Do you wait until the latest electronic gadget is on sale or buy it at full price the first day it comes out?

Young adults often have problems with how they handle money —but some older adults do too. Look around at all the advertising. There is always something tempting to buy, but Vanya found out that sometimes giving in to temptation can cost you big dollars in the long run.

THE SECRET

Vanya's Story

I'm a freshman this year at college, and at orientation there were companies giving away credit cards. Like most there, I signed up. They said I had a $500 a month limit. When I first got it, I thought that meant I had $500 a month to spend, so I started buying cute clothes or dinners out with friends or whatever. The credit card company just kept raising my limit. And then I started getting the bills. Now it's halfway through the year, and I owe them $2,500.

I DIDN'T EVEN KNOW CREDIT CARDS HAD DIFFERENT RATES!

I didn't know to ask about fees or the interest rate. I ended up paying a lot on both. And I didn't understand that the monthly payment would keep going up as the amount I owe went up. Then I learned if I missed a payment it could be reported to the credit bureaus, which might keep me from getting credit I might need later for school loans.

Now, I'm not sure where I'll get the money to pay them off. I'm looking for a part-time job, but it's hard to find one that pays much in a college town.

When I told my dad, he was really disappointed in the way I'd handled the credit. He told me to shred that card, and I did. And he said once this card was paid off, if I wanted to get a credit card to call him, and he'd help me find a better deal. I didn't even know credit cards had different rates!

UNLOCKING THE SECRET

Money is a real part of life for everyone—young and old. Unfortunately, bad habits with money that we develop when we are young often follow us through life unless we grow up financially and become wise about money and its uses. I have marveled at how even my six-year-old son has a concern about money. He asked me once, in between questions about God and life, why green pieces of paper and shiny coins seem to be so important to people. I explained that money is a tool we use to trade for things we want. As I see him collecting coins from around the house, or asking to keep the change, negotiating tasks for rewards, or wanting to set up a lemonade and cookie stand, I realize he is trying to figure out how to obtain this seemingly important tool for himself. Right now, his main or only source of income is me, his mom. But I know it's good for him to learn about money, even as young as he is.

> "My parents give me everything I need. If I need money for something, I just ask my mom. I figure I'll learn about that later on, or let my boyfriend pay for things."—Joleen

It's easy, when you're a teen to be like Joleen, to let your parents handle all the money in your life. But sooner or later you'll have to learn this for yourself. It's best to ask for your parents to help you learn to work with money now. If you don't, it will only cause headaches for you later on.

YOU MIGHT BE SURPRISED BY HOW MUCH YOU SPEND AND WHAT YOU SPEND YOUR MONEY ON.

One way to learn to work with money is to get a small notebook and write down where every penny you spend goes. You might be surprised by how much you spend and what you spend your money on.

Another way to learn about money is to find out what it would cost to live out some of your dreams. Perhaps you hope to move away from home into your own apartment when you graduate. Guess how much you think your apartment would cost. Then create a budget. Break down your budget by expense. For example, what would you guess the cost for each of the following to be?

- Food
- Utilities & rent
- Cleaning supplies
- Furniture
- Taxes

- Medical expenses
- Car expenses
- Insurance
- Clothes
- A night out with friends

Now ask a parent or mentor to look over your budget and see if you left any expenses out. Finally, find out the actual price of apartments and expenses in the area where you'd like to live. Is it more or less expensive than you thought? Can you find ways to lower your costs? How much would you need to earn to live in that apartment?

There are several Christian organizations committed to helping you understand money. One of them is Crown Financial Ministries. There are many resources and articles available on their Web site at www.crown.org, including a helpful article titled "Ten most asked questions about debt." For other sites, check out the Resources section that starts on page 217.

NO MORE SECRETS

If your secret is that you don't know much about money, let's do some work in this area right now. Take a few minutes to answer the following questions, either here or in your private notebook.

The things I spend most of my money on are

_____

_____

The things I'd like to do with my money someday are

Something I can do today to learn more about money is

Something I can do to earn money around my home or after school or during summer break is

In the next six months, my goal is to earn $_____ and save $_____.

SECRET STRENGTH

"The kingdom of heaven is like a man who was going to another place for a visit. Before he left, he called for his servants and told them to take care of his things while he was gone. He gave one servant five bags of gold, another servant two bags of gold, and a third servant one bag of gold, to each one as much as he could handle. Then he left. The servant who got five bags went quickly to invest the money and earned five more bags."
—*MATTHEW 25:14–16*

I know this sounds crazy—but it feels good when I cut myself.

do you cut yourself with razors or scratch yourself with other sharp objects until you bleed? Do you know anyone who does? Do you burn your skin or pick your scars? Do you hit yourself or bite yourself until you bruise? For a long time, many can hide these self-inflicted wounds from family and friends—until someone sees the scars and tells before the cutter or self-harmer can seriously hurt herself.

The question you might be asking is, why would anyone deliberately injure herself? There are numerous reasons why individuals use self-injury. However, most don't know why they start or how they came up with the idea, but find that they get relief from self-inflicted harm. In many cases, something traumatic happened in their lives that makes them feel overwhelmed with torturing emotions, and they don't know what to do or how to cope. Cutting and burning are the most common forms of self-injury,* and we know there are more girls who cut than boys. Cutting makes them feel in control.

---

* Jerusha Clark with Dr. Earl Henslin, *Inside A Cutter's Mind* (NavPress 2007).

THE SECRET

Aimee's Story

I remember wanting to kill myself as early as age 11, but I don't remember much of anything before that. I was always afraid of attempting suicide, failing, then having to live through the aftermath of everyone finding out. I didn't want to go through that.

I started cutting when I was about 13. I wanted to see if I had the nerve to cut myself, to make myself bleed, before I tried slitting my wrists. I was always thinking ahead. I cut the top of my wrists with a box cutter, maybe eight to ten times, but they didn't bleed at first, at least not until I went outside and noticed the dark red lines forming.

Somehow seeing the cuts calmed me. Because I had done this to myself, I felt in control. I kept cutting the rest of that summer and throughout my freshman year of high school until January. In January, I gave a suicide note to my friend. He had always been there for me, talked to me, and I felt like he deserved to know what I was planning to do and why I was doing it.

But I made the mistake of giving him the note too soon. I don't know why I did. Maybe I was subconsciously trying to make him stop me. I don't know. He went to the counselors at school, and my parents found out about every-thing—including that I cut. I was put into a behavioral hospital for nine days on a suicide watch. I got out of the hospital and went on a ton of different medica-tions for the next couple of years before finally getting off of them completely.

My parents think that I stopped cutting the day I went into the hospital at age 14, but I didn't stop until right before age 17. I was able to quit for two years, but then I started again when I was thrown into a situation beyond my control. The new situation was too much for me to handle and brought up too many old memories and issues that I had pushed down deep. So I relapsed.

With every day that goes by, I realize that I can't overcome this on my own, but I have a hard time asking for help. I hate what I have become. I hate living a secret and lying to everyone—but I can't stop. Even if I did manage to quit cutting, there are still the scars on my arms. I'm afraid I will be living this lie for the rest of my life, covering up scars and making excuses.

> **Some feelings associated with cutting include:**
> * Hurt
> * Rejection
> * Desperation
> * Emptiness
> * Anger
> * Rage
>
> —from "Cutting," September 2007, *TeensHealth*, Nemours Foundation

UNLOCKING THE SECRET

Cutting secrets such as Aimee's—along with all forms of self-injury—are a rising trend among young women today. Cutters or self-injurers are often intelligent, reflective, sensitive individuals who feel emotionally misunderstood or not taken seriously, or feel a huge gap between what they feel they must live up to for others versus what churns for them internally. They use their bodies to communicate what is too difficult to say. They cut themselves to help cope with, release, or rise above their emotional desperation or numbing deadness—to feel alive, real, or that they exist at all. Some use the physical pain and others the sight of the wound to divert their attention or make manageable this

8% of the young women we surveyed said **1** of their **top 5 secrets** is **cutting**.

deep emotional pain, although it only offers temporary relief from the internal chaos or difficult life circumstances they experience. The blade, the blood, the cut, the sensation, the ritual are seducing and become habit-forming and addictive.

Since cutters usually hide their scars, the signs are not always obvious. Most are not attention-seeking, but are silently screaming for help. Some signs to look for include a series of perfect slashes on the arms or legs, unexplained burns or bruises, clumps of missing hair, or someone who wears winter clothing to cover her arms and legs, even in warm weather.

If you are cutting or someone you know is cutting, talk to someone. It is okay to ask for help. There are also resources that can help you. For additional information, refer to the Resources section that starts on page 217.

Tara wrote a poem about her secret. It shows us that whatever situation we are in, we can cry out to God, for he will help through even the most painful times in our lives.

> ### Desperation
> *Here I am Lord.*
> *I'm crying out.*
> *Because I know that*
> *All I need is You.*
> *Through the trials*
> *And my storms ahead,*
> *I know you'll lead me through.*
> *But I am crying out*
> *In desperation.*
> *Lord, please*
> *Just show me what to do.*
> *—Tara*

NO MORE SECRETS

If your secret is cutting or self-inflicted harm, let's do some work in this area right now. Take a few minutes to answer the following questions here or in your private notebook.

The situation in my life that's most chaotic right now is

_____

_____

_____

_____

_____

When that chaotic situation happens, the emotions I feel most are
(Check any that apply.)

1. ___Rage		8. ___Fear	
2. ___Helplessness		9. ___Rejection	
3. ___Frustration		10. ___Insecurity	
4. ___Loneliness		11. ___Jealousy	
5. ___Despair		12. _____	
6. ___Tiredness		(other emotion)	
7. ___Annoyance			

If you are feeling any of the emotions on this list, talk with someone who can help you develop skills to cope with chaotic situations.

The times or situations when I most often feel like hurting myself are

_____

_____

The relief I am seeking from cutting myself is

_____

Write down the negative statements you make about yourself. Are these statements always true? Now write down an opposite, more loving response you might give to someone else or God might say to you. For example,

"I blew it again. I never do anything right."	to	"Everyone makes mistakes; it's okay to not be perfect," or "I can't control all outcomes, and sometimes, like last week, I do get it right."

SECRET STRENGTH

"Jesus turned and saw the woman and said, 'Be encouraged, dear woman. You are made well because you believed.' And the woman was healed from that moment on."—MATTHEW 9:22

If I were thinner, I'd be happier and more likeable.

angie tried every diet that exists. Then she began binging and throwing up. Soon she was on a weight-loss rollercoaster that caused her health problems and didn't keep her weight down for very long. Food controlled Angie. The solution to her problem with food had always been nearby; she'd just chosen to overlook it.

THE SECRET

Angie's Story

My weight problem started when I was about eight years old. A thin girl around my age told me to my face that I was fat, and I remember how badly she hurt my feelings.

Most of my family is overweight. Dealing with my weight problem was an ongoing struggle throughout my childhood and teen years. Even when I wasn't hungry I ate, but at the same time I was extremely eager to lose the weight. I've always been an emotional binge eater with an obsession for food. I was binging so much that both my mind and body didn't know what was going on. Food became my comfort. I ate when I was happy and when I was sad. Sometimes I ate so much that my stomach would ache in agony. At times I had to unbutton my pants, make my way to a couch, or lie down. Needless to say, two hours later I would be right back at it.

I was really depressed over my indulgence with food, which was often. I forced myself to go on a diet. I took the latest diet pills and made false promises to myself and to everyone else that I would stay on that particular diet and lose the weight for good. But after a few days, I always clung to the food and would get into the same vicious cycle. It was as if I were in an abusive relationship with food. I loved it, but I hated how it made me feel. Food controlled me, and I allowed it to do so. I overate all of the time, and this cycle went on for years.

It was pathetic. I was embarrassed, and I felt horrible about myself. I knew exactly how I would feel if I ate too much, but I did it anyway. I knew what it would do to my thighs, butt, waist, and hips—but I continued to overeat.

At one point, I read that Albert Einstein supposedly said, "Insanity is doing the same thing over and over again and expecting a different result." I began to wonder if I were a crazy person with an eating problem. It was so out of control that I knew I had to make a lifestyle change—so I did.

It was extremely hard, but with some help I started to get my life under control. I started drinking plenty of water and exercising every day. Sometimes that exercise might be simply parking farther away from the school entrance so that I had a longer walk, but it counted.

And I began writing about my struggles and all of the other things in my life, which has helped me in getting my weight problem under control and in putting everything into perspective. When I saw my feelings written down on paper, it helped me realize what was really going on in my life. Writing has become my therapy, along with reading a lot of self-help books, and keeping the fridge and cabinets stocked with healthy food. I've always enjoyed snacking a lot, but now I make sure I eat healthy snacks including fruits, nuts, vegetables, yogurt, and low-cal and low-fat snacks.

I'm maintaining a healthy weight. I feel better physically and mentally. It *wasn't an easy fix, because there is not an easy fix. And I don't think of this as a diet; I think of it as the way I should have always been eating.*

Do I ever sometimes eat something really calorie-laden? Rarely, but I do. Then I go right back to eating properly. I tell my story because many other young women allow food to control their lives. If food is controlling your life, I encourage you to make a change. Make a change and make your life better.

UNLOCKING THE SECRET

Eating disorders are very serious. Anorexia and bulimia primarily affect people starting in their teens and twenties, but studies report both disorders in children as young as six and in individuals as old as seventy-six. In my practice as a psychologist, I have met with girls who have started their eating disorder at age nine and have worked with women who still struggle with binging and purging going into their sixties. An Anorexia Nervosa and Related Eating Disorders, Inc. (ANRED) report shows that more than half of teenage girls are on, or think they should be on, diets. Without treatment, up to 20 percent of people with serious eating disorders die. With treatment, that number falls to 2–3 percent.

I remember being amazed at hearing my daughter and her friends picking apart their bodies while only in the first grade. Self image, body image, and the need to be perfect or the fear of our imperfection starts very young. It starts in our disordered thinking, just as it did for Eve when the serpent tempted her that she could be perfect like God. We all are like Eve.

In my work with girls and women of all ages who struggle with all forms of eating disorders, I am hopeful, as eating disorders don't have to be lifelong. Sadly, not all end well, and my heart is grieved for those I have known or heard about who have died from these disorders. No one can abuse her body for long and expect to not suffer adverse consequences.

Eating disorders have often been called the "good girl" disorder, because they often affect respectable girls who are pleasing and cooperative, who are not acting out with defiant behavior. Instead they are really acting-in against themselves, and for all of their outward pleasantries, they are inwardly self-loathing and filled with emotion. Girls often get into eating disorder behaviors out of curiosity, or when fears about themselves or growing up are triggered. They see how others have gotten thin or hear about purging tactics. Initial triggers might be about their bodies, looks, perfection, fear of not being good enough, being teased by peers, or a life that generally feels out of control.

Stacy writes about teasing between girls who already are self-conscience about their bodies and appearance.

Girls are definitely in an awkward stage when they're teenagers, and now body image is key. Trying to look good, girls may be experimenting with makeup and don't fully understand how to apply it. They may put on the wrong shade (which makes them look orange) or too much (which makes it look really thick). As a result, they get teased or called names.

Teenagers are always growing and will lose and gain weight at different times and rates. Some girls tend to have bigger breasts—and the guys give more attention to those girls. Then other girls will be mean and make up rumors about the girls with larger breasts being "sluts," because they don't get the same attention as the bigger-breasted girls. All girls are awkward about their bodies at this age. And girls will make mean stuff up about other girls to make themselves feel better. All of us girls do all we can to avoid being the target of such ridicule, even if it means hurting ourselves.

Those who struggle with anorexia sometimes want to keep

their bodies looking like little girls' bodies, so they create rigidity in their lives to maintain control. Restrictive eating and behavior gives them a feeling of mastery or success. Or they think that if they can survive on little and have few needs, they can reach a life of perfect self-control. If they achieve this, they believe they can keep bad things from happening to them.

Anorexia tends to be hard to keep secret over time. Some girls who start with anorexia flip into bulimia, using a combination of binging, restricting, fasting, and purging behaviors. Bulimia also can destroy a female's body with the inconsistent and extreme binge-purge cycle. I've heard girls and women say things like, "I used to have to stick my finger or my toothbrush down my throat, but now as soon as I lean over the toilet it just comes up," or "Food is always there like a best friend. I eat even in the middle of the night. But then I feel sick and hate myself for eating and have to get it out. The vomiting makes me dizzy and it's painful, but I know I have to do it to get relief. Afterward, I am wrung out, and I hate myself even more."

A person's struggle with eating has little to do with food. It is, however, about a hunger, a longing, an emptiness. Some refer to it as "love hunger" that gets all mixed up with feelings about growing up, feeling little, separating from parents (especially Mom), and control or lack of control with family or in life. How a young woman feels about herself affects her core feelings of purpose, image, and worth. Genesis 1:27 talks about being created in God's image, and that means you are perfect in his eyes. He created you uniquely and with a purpose. But in this present-day world, we will not realize that perfection. Someday we will have perfect bodies but not now, and our task is to learn to accept and love ourselves in our imperfection.

In 1 Corinthians 6:12–13, the Bible says, "'I am allowed to do all things,' but not all things are good for me to do. 'I am allowed to do all things,' but I will not let anything make me its slave. 'Food is for the

stomach, and the stomach for food,' but God will destroy them both."
I like the food analogy used here. It goes on to talk about sexual sin,
but the emphasis is in using your body, the body God gave you for
his glory. "You should know that your body is a temple for the Holy
Spirit who is in you. You have received the Holy Spirit from God. So
you do not belong to yourselves, because you were bought by God
for a price. So honor God with your bodies" (1 Corinthians 6:19–20).

If your secret is with food, ask God to show you what is real
and ask for help before you get too far down the road. Don't be
afraid to ask for help. Seek God. Tell someone you trust. And seek
professional help.

Main Types of Eating Disorders

There are three main types of eating disorders studied by the experts
and listed in the DSM-IV-TR (*Diagnostic and Statistical Manual of
Mental Disorders*, 4th edition / training edition):

Anorexia nervosa.
A refusal to maintain minimally normal body weight for your age
and height. Intense fear of becoming fat regardless of size. Denial
of seriousness of low body weight and distortion of body shape and
weight influencing a negative evaluation of self. Amenorrhea can
occur, which is the loss of three consecutive menstrual cycles.

Bulimia nervosa.
Characterized by repeated episodes of binge-eating, followed by
self-induced vomiting, misuse of laxatives or diuretics or other med-

ications, fasting, or excessive exercise. Feeling out of control while eating in this diet-binge-purge cycle that occurs at least twice a week for a three-month period. Distortion of body shape and weight influencing a negative evaluation of self.

Compulsive overeating.

Now referred to as binge eating disorder it is characterized by larger-than-normal amounts eaten in short periods of time (within a 2-hour time frame), followed by physical discomfort and emotional distress, but no purging.

Factors

No one factor causes an eating disorder. Following is a list of the factors that are sometimes attributed to each disorder.

Anorexia

- Fear of growing up
- Inability to separate from the family
- Need to please or be liked
- Perfectionism
- Need to control
- Need for attention
- Lack of self-esteem

- High family expectations
- Parental dieting
- Family discord
- Temperament—often described as the "perfect child"
- Teasing about weight and body shape

Bulimia

- Difficulty regulating mood
- Sexual abuse

- Availability and indulgence of food

- More impulsive—sometimes with shoplifting, substance abuse, etc.
- Emphasis on thinness as the ideal for beauty
- Role of the media
- Family dysfunction
- Obesity and reaction to the larger body size

Used by permission from the Anorexia Nervosa and Related Eating Disorders, Inc. (ANRED), www.anred.com. For more information, contact ANRED or the National Association of Anorexia Nervosa and Associated Disorders, www.anad.org.

NO MORE SECRETS

Is an eating disorder your secret? Let's do some work in this area right now. Take a few minutes to answer the following questions, either here or in your private notebook.

Answer the following questions.

(Circle yes or no.)

1. I eat too much and continue to eat until I feel sick. **Yes/No**
2. I skip meals. **Yes/No**
3. I skip meals because I think I'm too fat. **Yes/No**
4. I exercise ALL THE TIME. **Yes/No**
5. I'm obsessed with being thin. **Yes/No**
6. I'm terrified of gaining weight. **Yes/No**
7. I often feel out of control and can't stop eating. **Yes/No**
8. I throw up after I eat. **Yes/No**
9. I try to diet but always fail. **Yes/No**

Use these questions as a simple guide but not the final word. If you answered "yes" to any of these questions, you may or may not have an eating disorder. If you answered "yes" to two or more of these questions and spend a high percentage of time worrying about these things, an eating disorder is more likely. Either way, take the time to talk over your weight and body concerns with a trusted adult.

My prayer is

> *God,*
> *Help me to see myself as you see me. I place my struggle in your hands and I am asking for help. I pray that you will help me gain control, to recover, and to honor you with my body. I ask that you bring the people and resources into my life that I need. Amen.*

SECRET STRENGTH

"So brothers and sisters, since God has shown us great mercy, I beg you to offer your lives as a living sacrifice to him. Your offering must be only for God and pleasing to him, which is the spiritual way for you to worship. Do not be shaped by this world; instead be changed within by a new way of thinking. Then you will be able to decide what God wants for you; you will know what is good and pleasing to him and what is perfect."
—ROMANS 12:1–2

I don't know what I believe about God.

*t*he most important thing in life is your relationship with God. But sometimes it can be difficult to know what you truly believe—especially when you or your family or friends are facing some type of crisis. As you read through this chapter, you'll find that the girls who shared their stories didn't live perfect lives and sometimes questioned their faith as Alisha did.

THE SECRET

Alisha's Story

I grew up going to church. My dad, stepmom, and grandma were strong Christians and very active in our local church.

I've always been pretty intellectual, and by my early teens, I started thinking about things like I'm not sure where I am with my faith, and How can I know God is real? I couldn't grasp that God was real because I couldn't physically touch or see him.

My grandmother was a huge influence in my life. I knew how important her faith was to her. And I admired the way she not only believed but lived her faith.

For her it was real, but I just didn't have that same feeling. She would say that if I studied God's Word and really thought about it, I'd begin believing. She spent a lot of time helping me and encouraging me to talk to other Christians.

My journey took me a long time, but by listening to my doubts, my grandma helped me draw closer to God and discover him for myself.

"I've been raised Catholic, but I don't think I'm a Christian anymore. My mom is a Christian, and so is my boyfriend. But I'm not sure what I believe about faith."—Devon

"I believe in God, but my youth pastor's baby just died. How could God let something so bad like that happen? It makes me wonder if there really is a God, or if there is, if he loves us like he says he does."—Lyndi

"I've been homeschooled all my life and God is very important to my family. We think that the modern culture is harmful and will try to press us into its evil mold. But sometimes I go to a youth group where the kids don't think modern culture is wrong, or at least they don't act like it. A lot of them listen to all sorts of secular music and watch MTV. The girls wear a lot of makeup. I know two guys who drink beer. Isn't Christian behavior important? I think God wants us to act and behave righteously."—Brianna

"My best friend this year is an exchange student from India. She's a Hindu and worships a lot of different gods. I went with her to a temple once, and she came with me to youth group. I don't think I believe what she does. In fact I'm sure I don't. But I don't know what to say to her. Jesus Christ says he's the way, the truth, and the life. But I don't know how to tell her that."—Madeline

UNLOCKING THE SECRET

When your friends, parents, or other people you're close to don't hold the same Christian values you do, it can be tough. When you experience loss or have something bad happen, it's not uncommon to ask God why those things happened. When others don't hold the same cultural values or beliefs you do, it can be hard to discern what's truly important.

Those things are all part of the faith journey. There are times in our lives when our faith is going to be tested, and there are going to be other times in life when we will need to figure out different aspects of our faith. Exposure to different beliefs and values is not a threat to your faith but an opportunity to think through and really know what you believe is right for you as a Christian. God is not afraid of your doubts, nor does he want you to be. He will sit with you in that doubting place—just ask him to help you learn and to bring the right people into your life who can help you discern what's true. God allows us to go through difficult situations and experiences so that he can strengthen us. He wants our faith to continually grow. If we never faced challenges, we'd always stay in the same place.

One of the best things you can do when you have questions about your faith is to meet with other believers who can help you sort through what you believe. Ask your youth sponsor for some time to sit and talk, or make an appointment with your pastor to ask him all the hard questions you want to. Keep reading the Bible. God's word is the source of all truth.

The stories of the teens in this chapter make me think of the words in 1 Peter 1:5–7: "God's power protects you through your faith until salvation is shown to you at the end of time. This makes you very happy, even though now for a short time different kinds of troubles may make you sad. These troubles come to prove that your faith is pure. This purity of faith is worth more than gold, which can be proved to be pure by fire but will ruin. But the purity of your faith will bring you praise and glory and honor when Jesus Christ is shown to you."

NO MORE SECRETS

If your secret is that you're figuring out what you believe, that's okay. Faith is often a process or a journey. It's not formed instantly. There might be times when you need to be quiet and let God speak to you by his Word. There might be other times when you need to use words to defend your faith. Still other times you might need to pull out your Bible and study through a passage to figure out what it means.

Let's do some work in this area right now. Read through the poem "Words of Hope." Then take a few minutes to answer the following questions, either here or in your private notebook.

Words of Hope

When you feel
All hope is gone
And your soul
In chains is bound,
Go to the place
Where hope is found,
Where sin's erased,
Where shame he takes,
Gives you a new name—
A place

Where souls are purged.
A place
Where hearts emerge
To rise above flesh,
Quench every man's thirst
Where hope lives,
Hope is in his Word
—Celeste

How is God working in your life right now?

_____

_____

_____

What challenges are you facing in regard to your faith?

_____

_____

_____

Where can you go to get positive input about your relationship with God? How is God using your faith to influence others?

_____

_____

_____

Name some of the people God has put into your life whom, you can encourage to have a closer relationship with God.

_____

_____

How might God be using you in those situations?

_____

_____

_____

_____

Name some of the people God has used in your life to speak to you or strengthen your faith?

_____

_____

SECRET STRENGTH

"But respect Christ as the holy Lord in your hearts. Always be ready to answer everyone who asks you to explain about the hope you have."—1 PETER 3:15

Sometimes I want to kill myself.

When life gets really hard, some people begin to think that the only way out is to take their own life. The chaos around us is so bad it seems like the only hope is suicide.

I just want to say very clearly that thoughts of suicide are always from the enemy. If you (or a friend) are thinking of killing yourself, don't do it. Wait. Seek help immediately. God can use others to bring you to a hopeful place again. Carly got the help she needed, and so can you.

THE SECRET

Carly's Story

My story begins when I was 15. My parents were alcoholics and had no use for my brother and me. They constantly told us we were both "accidents." They would sit around and watch television. It was my older brother who went to the store, made us food, taught me how to cook, and kept the house clean.

Even though Mom always complained about Dad drinking too much, she would drink with him, and when my dad was totally drunk, my mom would get real quiet and start weeping. My dad hated that and usually got angry and started cussing at all of us, threatening to leave. And there were lots of times when he would get really mad and become violent toward any of us who got in his way.

Then at a school fair day, I met a youth pastor from a neighboring town near where I lived. He invited me to attend a youth rally at a local park that his church was putting on. I decided I wanted to go and asked my brother if he'd go with me. After attending the rally and meeting other kids, we began going to the "lost & found" youth club at the pastor's church. It was really fun and a good break from home. After several months, both my brother and I accepted Christ as our Savior.

However in the upcoming months, my walk with Christ grew weak. I was really sad when my brother got accepted to the army, and soon he was stationed in a war zone. I worried that I'd never see him again, and my living situation became more stressful.

One day my father got into an argument with me when I made the mistake of saying something about his alcoholism. He started to swing at me, and I just barely got out of the way when he tripped and fell into a cabinet. I hid in my room until he calmed down. When he got up, he told my mom to call the local sheriff's department and tell them that I was out of control and needed to be in juvy. They came out to the house and saw

I WAS SO TIRED AND DEPRESSED THAT I TRIED TO KILL MYSELF.

for themselves that my mom was a wreck and my dad had passed out drunk. The sheriff told my mom that they could not do anything about the situation.

I was so tired and depressed that I tried to kill myself. But when I cut my wrists, I went into an anxiety attack and passed out. The next morning I woke up with blood all over my arms. I cleaned it off, put on a long-sleeve sweatshirt to cover the cuts, and went to church.

After the youth club was over, my pastor asked me what was wrong. At first, I told him nothing. He asked to see my wrists. I was really scared.

Then I told him that I felt like no one cared about me. He told me that he had been praying and kept feeling God wanted him to check on me. Wow! I freaked out.

The youth pastor told me that God will always care about me. He offered to help me find a counselor. I agreed to talk with a counselor, but I didn't have any money. Before the end of that Sunday, he had made me an appointment with a counselor who would not charge me anything. I also joined Alateen (a support group for teens whose lives have been affected by someone's alcoholism). Through Alateen I found out I was not alone.

... THOSE SUICIDAL THOUGHTS I HAD WERE FROM THE DEVIL

I still have suicidal thoughts that run through my mind. But when they come, I start to pray. And when I pray, I remember that those suicidal thoughts I had were from the devil. So I continue to pray and cling to Christ, knowing that with God all things are possible.

UNLOCKING THE SECRET

When life is tough and you feel all alone, or feel like no one understands, it is easy to get down or depressed. Depression can lead to distorted thinking, like telling yourself things that just aren't true.

The longer you keep things to yourself, the worse you tend to feel. Sometimes it feels like you have no options or choices to change your situation. If you feel trapped, sometimes you can wish to be out of your pain so badly that the only way out seems to be to end it all. Suicidal thoughts and feelings can come and go. Suicidal attempts can lead to permanent outcomes that are no solution at all. When you no longer have hope, that is the time to allow others to have hope for you.

Many times people who are suicidal have additional secrets. If your secret is that you or someone you know is using alcohol or drugs, see Secret #21 on page 176. If your secret is that you are depressed, see Secret #8 on page 62.

Living through tough times is never easy, but you can survive those times when you reach out to God and to trusted people. God does not want you to take your own life. He made you, and he hears and understands your desperation—even when it feels like he is not listening. Don't allow situations, other people, or evil to determine the value of your life. Nothing is so great that he isn't greater still, and God can always bring good from bad situations.

> "To everyone thinking about suicide, do what I do: Take a break, just walk away long enough to take a deep breath. It gives me the time to realize the seriousness of what I was thinking. I will ask myself, 'Is this what I really want?' Then I call someone I can talk to. There is always someone who is willing to help."—Alyssa

NO MORE SECRETS

If your secret is that you have thoughts of suicide, you need to talk to someone you can trust. There may be a lot of pain in your life, but suicide is never the answer.

If you are feeling suicidal or sometimes have suicidal thoughts, following are some things you can do in the moment:

- **Keep a list**—to refer to (or look at pictures) of people who would be deeply hurt by you taking your life, and remember to include God.
- **Be with someone**—at least one other person, and *do not* stay alone when these thoughts are present.
- **Change your surroundings**—go outside, to the mall, for a ride, to a church group, or to a friend's house.
- **Distract yourself**—talk to a friend or call your grandma, your aunt, cousin, or any family member; watch a movie; exercise; play with and care for a pet.

If you have a plan to act on suicidal feelings or know a friend who does . . .

- **Call right away**—a parent, a relative, a mentor, a pastor, a teacher, or a friend until you reach someone.
- **Get immediate help**—
  - The number for the USA National Suicide Hotline is **1-800-suicide**, or **1-800-273-TALK**.
  - Go to your computer and type in key search words: **Teen Suicide Hotline**.
  - **Call 9-1-1** if you (or a friend) are in the act of or about to hurt yourself.
- **Develop a plan for living**—let others help you by sharing your secret pain and getting into counseling with an experienced professional; also start meeting with Christians regularly who can pour God's love into you.

Take a few minutes to answer the following questions, either here or in your private notebook.

Have you ever felt so down or trapped that you've wanted to end your life? If so, write about that time and how you overcame those feelings.

_____

_____

_____

_____

_____

What if your best friend felt that way and came to you, how would you respond? (Read "Stepping into a Secret-Free Life: Step 3—You can't trust everyone, but you can trust someone," on page 83.)

_____

_____

_____

Can you think of a time when someone else's advice helped you out? How did it make a difference in your life?

_____

_____

_____

Think of a time when God used you to speak to someone else. What happened?

_____

_____

SECRET STRENGTH

"Why am I so sad?
  Why am I so upset?
I should put my hope in God
  and keep praising him,
  my Savior and my God."—PSALM 42:11

HOW TO STOP HIDING YOUR SECRET

(and why that's a good thing).

*t*he goal is not to air all your dirty laundry for the whole world to see, but to stop allowing your secrets to define you. Your goal is to put an end to the secrets that hinder you in your relationships and keep you from living your life to its fullest. When you keep the truth hidden, it usually means you're not pursuing solutions to your problems, which allows your troubles to grow and become worse.

It's not that you never want to keep anything private. As I said earlier, it's okay to have secrets. The point in sharing your harmful secrets is that you don't need to carry them around like weights. Even though you can have the knowledge of a particular truth about yourself, it doesn't have to weigh you down.

There are three ways that you can safely stop hiding and begin to live as God truly meant you to live.

1. Tell your secret to yourself.

This may sound obvious, but the first step in telling any secret is to be honest with yourself about it—and keep being honest with yourself about it. Do not shrug off your secret as if it's no big deal. If something is causing you concern, then it's valid.

Earlier in the book, I asked you to take a moment and name your secret. Sometimes this is harder than it looks. Once you get into the habit of keeping a secret, other secrets can begin stacking on top of it. When that happens, it can be hard to recognize the original secret.

But the first step to releasing the pressure of that secret is to tell the secret to yourself. Keep telling it—that's why I mention this step again here. This first step is an important milestone, and if you haven't done it already, I encourage you to do it now.

2. Tell your secret to God.

Perhaps the single most freeing step you can take is to completely lay your secret before God. It may be a *confession* or it may be more like a pouring out of your pain and sorrow. Whatever it is, if you start by allowing God's light into your dark places, you can immediately experience some of the pressure lifting. When you acknowledge that you're not alone and that God wants to hear you, and when you ask him to sit with you in your pain, he's faithful to do just that.

3. Tell your secret to a trusted friend or adult.

Somebody close to you needs to know this truth about you. Sometimes there may be a close friendship that hasn't grown because of your inability to be vulnerable and open, so you need to take this person into your confidence. Perhaps you need to be real with your parents, or maybe you and a sibling have issues that could begin healing with the two of you talking. It's up to you to decide whether to share with a friend or family member, a teacher, a mentor, a youth pastor or youth leader, or sometimes a counselor in your school or an association such as those listed in the Resources section on page 217.

- -

"Confess your sins to each other and pray for each other so God can heal you. When a believing person prays, great things happen."—JAMES 5:16

- -

Talking to a counselor can often be a very good thing. A counselor can act as a safe third party to your secret, help you acknowledge the hidden parts of yourself, and determine who else in your life needs to be allowed inside. If you're feeling especially burdened by your secret—if it's ruling your life in some way—then I encourage you to consider seeking a safe, professional counseling environment in which to explore it.

A counselor will also know about support groups that provide an opportunity for interaction with people going through similar situations who can relate to your struggles. These groups offer the opportunity to talk openly with your peers. Sometimes these groups might even meet in your school.

If your school doesn't have a counselor, talk to the school nurse or ask a teacher for help. For other counseling centers and support groups check out the Resources section on page 217.

How will the person I tell react?

After you figure out whom to tell your secret to, the next concern is how will the person react? Sometimes the people you share your secret with will react in a way you don't expect.

- The person might remain calm. He or she might have already suspected your secret.
- The person could be relieved because he or she knew something was wrong and imagined something far worse than your secret
- The person might need a little time to think about it, or might be disappointed.
- The person might even be shocked. That happens.

Sometimes it takes awhile for the person to work through the seriousness of what you've just told them. All of that is okay. Just give the situation time. Remember: You know the secret, and you've chosen when to share the secret, but this is all new to the person you're talking to—so give him or her some time to think about what you said. If your secret is a sin or mistake, then admitting it means facing that it's not something that will make others feel good either. After all, isn't that why you were keeping it secret in the first place—to avoid those bad feelings. But getting through the bad feelings makes room for the good.

For instance, I know one parent who was very upset when her daughter, a head cheerleader and homecoming queen who seemed to be doing everything perfectly, told her she was having sex. The

56% said it is *sometimes difficult to talk about how they feel*. **14%** said it is *often difficult*.

mom was angry, embarrassed, worried for her daughter, and did not know what to do. That mother had to come to terms with the fact that her daughter was not perfect, that she had made a mistake, and that she as a parent may also have let her daughter down. She had to love her daughter right where she was, and stop putting her own wishes on her daughter. It took the mother awhile to get to that place, but eventually she did, and she was glad her daughter had come to her so they could deal with it together and have a more real relationship. You might be convinced that your parents would never get to a place of accepting you in spite of your mistakes, but give them a little credit. Many parents might be willing to grow more than you think.

No matter what their reaction, remember that they won't die from disappointment and neither will you. After the initial surprise and once people are aware of the situation, they can be more real and honest with you and can begin seeking helpful solutions.

"I've told someone!"

Once you've told your secret to someone, try to stay calm during the person's initial reaction. You might even be prepared to ask the person if he or she would like to think about what you said and talk later. Then set a time to talk about it. The person's response might be much different than you expected. Once the person has had time to consider your secret, he or she may not be shocked at all, but may understand where you are and work with you toward a solution.

As I said earlier, if the person you tell doesn't listen or isn't willing to help you with your secret, go to the next person on your list or to a resource like the ones listed in the Resources section starting on page 217.

One step at a time.

This is the fourth step to living a secret-free life. Take some time to review your secret from the first section. Is that really your secret, or is it hiding your real secret? If it is your secret, write it again, either here or in your notebook. If it's not, write your real secret.

My secret is

_____

_____

I keep my secret hidden because

_____

_____

I'm going to share my secret with my friend _____ .

A trusted adult I will tell my secret to is _____ .

My prayer is

_____

_____

_____

_____

    Amen.

I desperately want to be loved.

*l*ove is a great thing. Love is a huge part of our lives. God created love, but sometimes love becomes a secret in our lives. We obsess about receiving love, about having someone to love, about having someone to love us back, about losing love, about gaining love, about being loved forever.

THE SECRET

Elizabeth's Story

When I found love, I became obsessed. Romantic love seemed from another world, exciting, mysterious, dangerous, and so adultlike. It was as if I finally got a small sip of water after crossing a desert. I wanted to be near him and smell his skin and clothes. I wanted to cry in front of him and tell him all of my stories. I found my value in his approval. I lived my days thinking only of when I could see him again. I hung my whole energy on this unbreakable bond.

And then the unthinkable happened: We broke up. I was confused. Suddenly, love was dangerous. At 17, I was convinced that if I tried to love again, I would lose myself, my dreams, my ambition, and my control.

When I closed the door to love, I thought I would become better in a lot of ways. I could say what I wanted and not be ashamed of my dreams. I could become stronger and more independent. The loneliness and discipline would teach me new ways to look at myself, at my time, and at other people. I would invest in friendships more, and I would learn how to have fun in a group. Without the burden of love, I would accomplish so much more.

Just as I thought, I am well on my way to achieving something big. I was forced to take another look at love. My cousin and her fiancée met in college. After they graduated, they married. Why are they still themselves, still individuals? They both have their own passions, desires, and goals, and they still hang out with the group.

Why do they seem satisfied and in the moment, mentally present, and invested even when they are not with each other? Shouldn't she be worried to do that, say this, and wear that? My sister completely changed when she fell in love and got married. She became a superwife, submissive, self-deprecating, and lost her edge. I wondered.

THEN I WENT IN MY ROOM, LAY ON MY BED, AND CRIED IN TRUE 17-YEAR-OLD FASHION.

Then I went in my room, lay on my bed, and cried in true 17-year-old fashion. I faced the desires I felt I could not control, desires I had sealed in a box. Maybe what I thought was love wasn't. Or maybe it was, and I just was not mature enough to balance it in my life.

What is love? Did I love him because I craved his voice and respected his character? Did I love him because he had a way of doing everyday things that made those things seem special? I've heard love is when you put someone else before yourself. What does that mean? As I mulled it over, I asked God to give me wisdom about it or at least some peace. I saw the love I desired. I saw that true love would not harm me, but would set me free.

"All I want is someone to hold hands with. I want so badly to walk across my school's campus holding a guy's hand, just as other girls do. There's this one guy, Russell, he's at the top of my list. But I don't think he notices me. At least not yet." —Sydney

"My boyfriend and I just broke up. I never want to be in love again." —Ariana

UNLOCKING THE SECRET

As we grow up, we start to notice members of the opposite sex. Then there comes a time when we start dating and taking a closer look at love, with all of its aches, pain, and glory.

Most of us experience our share of crushes throughout our tween, teen, and college years. Those wonderful romances can be exciting times, but love can also let us down. It's so easy to have hopes crushed.

Being "in love" or even "in like" are powerful emotions and important milestones as we grow up. We learn a lot about ourselves through these experiences. To see a reflection of ourselves in another person's eyes feels good. At first it is like looking in a mirror that shows us our ideal selves. This is why infatuation is like being drunk on love. It's when two people see each other as simply wonderful. Over time, more realistic views of ourselves and the other person are revealed, and incorporating our not-so-good parts and theirs into this ideal picture can cause the mirror to come crashing down. Learning to accept ours and other people's good and bad parts, and loving others and ourselves in spite of faults, is the maturing process of love.

No one becomes an expert at love and dating without going through those first vulnerable, awkward experiences of wondering if they are likable, lovable, and of interest to another person. Sometimes you can want that assurance of love and value so much that you are willing to do almost anything to get it and keep it. This is where some young women set themselves up for hurt by giving too much of their heart away too fast and their investment in the other person becomes out of balance. These women lose themselves to the *idea* of being in love more than the actual person and often put that ideal onto whomever they're currently dating.

If your whole being is wrapped up in maintaining your romance to the neglect of the rest of your life and it feels like you couldn't live without the relationship, or your relationship causes you to feel bad about yourself, or you judge your worth by being identified with your boyfriend—you are in an unhealthy situation. Dating does not mean giving up who you are or being addicted to a person. Healthy love doesn't isolate you or tear you down; it connects you to others and builds you up.

Dating is a great way to practice connecting ourselves to another person in partnership before we make that eventual lifetime commitment. Like conducting an experiment and learning the results before drawing up your conclusions—it's a way to get to know who you are in relation to another person and what types of people are the best fit for your personality.

Halfway through my senior year of high school I started dating a guy whom I had known through my church youth group. He was the "new guy" from another school—cute, friendly, and popular. Still lamenting over my last break-up months earlier, and not sure this new guy was for real, I didn't fall for his charm right away. Eventually, though, he got my attention; we clicked and started hanging out together. Over time I grew to really care about him and love him; he became my best friend. It was a sad day when we both left for college and had to be apart. On trips to visit each other, I recall being shocked at how many girls would comment to me about how lucky I was to be with such a cute, great guy! After what seemed like dozens of comments on multiple occasions, I turned to one unsuspecting girl and kindly said, "I don't think I'm exactly road kill, and he's pretty lucky to have me too." And I meant it.

Learning about and bettering ourselves through relationships is an important aspect of dating. Seeing our worth and what we have to offer is equally of value if not greater than finding that "perfect" guy.

While I didn't end up marrying this guy, we are still friends today. I think God used the relationship to help shape us both even though we weren't "the ones" ultimately for each other.

If you're not in love now and want to be, relax. God is the author of every good and perfect gift. He will bring love into your life in his timing. One of the best things you can do when you're not in love is become the person you need to be while you're waiting.

- Focus on your character.
- Develop strong friendships with people of both genders.
- Stop worrying about trying to get asked out; go out and have fun with groups of friends.
- Set high standards for whom you eventually date.
- Don't sell yourself short.
- Never compromise your beliefs and date the wrong guy just because you want to be loved.

If you've been in love and it's gone now, love can come again. It takes time and prayer for a good connection.

God has created us to love and to be loved. God expects us to love him first and then to love others. The Bible talks about that in Matthew 22:37–39: "Jesus answered, 'Love the Lord your God with all your heart, all your soul, and all your mind.' This is the first and most important command. And the second command is like the first: 'Love your neighbor as you love yourself.'"

NO MORE SECRETS

If your secret is wanting to be loved, let's do some work in that area right now. Take a few minutes to answer the following questions, either here or in your private notebook.

Think of a couple of people you like or have dated. What qualities do/did they possess that you like?

_____

_____

_____

_____

Are there any qualities you don't like about those you are dating or have dated?

_____

_____

_____

Is God a priority in any of their lives?

_____

_____

_____

Are there any ways you have been out of balance or had unhealthy expectations for dating?

_____

_____

Name five characteristics that you are looking for in someone you would like to date and eventually marry.

_____

_____

_____

_____

_____

> It is important to learn that others may give and receive love differently than you do. If you feel unloved, maybe you are just not seeing the love that is right before your eyes. The five love languages are words of affirmation, quality time, gifts, acts of service, and physical touch. —*Five Love Languages* by Dr. Gary Chapman

How you give and receive love in all types of relationships will give you awareness of what will be important to you in your romantic love relationships.

List some practical ways you can demonstrate God's love to others (read Colossians 3:12–14). For example,

- Be kind.
- Show others you care.
- Express gratitude.
- Share your thoughts and feelings.
- Give of your time and talents.
- _____
- _____
- _____

How does God show you how much he loves you? (Read John 3:16)

_____

_____

SECRET STRENGTH

"Love is patient and kind. Love is not jealous, it does not brag, and it is not proud. Love is not rude, is not selfish, and does not get upset with others. Love does not count up wrongs that have been done. Love takes no pleasure in evil but rejoices over the truth. Love patiently accepts all things. It always trusts, always hopes, and always endures."—1 CORINTHIANS 13:4–7

Someone has hurt me physically.

Physical abuse is when someone hits, kicks, slaps, chokes, bites, burns, pushes, or harms you in any way that involves your body being hurt. Some people think that being abused physically is a normal part of life. But it's not. It shouldn't be. If you are being physically abused by a parent, relative, boyfriend, or anybody else, seek help immediately. As Samantha learned, you do not have to be hurt.

THE SECRET

Samantha's Story

A friend and I were at an amusement park when we met Nate. He was smiling at me, gesturing for me to come over. I was shy, so I asked my friend to ask him for his number. She did and he gladly obliged. Nate and I talked over the phone a couple of times, and we set a date to meet again at the same amusement park. At the time, it seemed like a typical relationship for a teenager, but that quickly changed.

On our third meeting, we met a group of friends at the amusement park.

At one point, I was walking a little fast and Nate's friend started talking to me. Nate did not like that at all. He grabbed my arm, jerked me toward him, and swatted me on the behind. He said, "Why did you leave me?"

At first I thought it was odd that he reacted like that. But then I thought it felt good because I thought it meant he really liked me. I thought, Wow, this is great. As time went on, we continued to meet at various places.

One Saturday night stands out in my mind. His mom drove up to the mall and dropped us off so we could hang out there and go to a movie. As we were walking through the mall and I was looking around, I happened to look in the direction of another young man. Nate immediately began yelling and screaming at me in the middle of the crowded mall. I was so embarrassed. People were staring at us, so I walked away.

About ten minutes later he found me. Then he grabbed me and slapped me in the face. He must have called his mom to come pick us up right after I'd walked away, because by the time he found me she had arrived. When I got into the car, he was even more furious at me and called me a b****, and he punched me in the mouth. I remember tasting blood and saying, "You made me bleed." I was crying and screaming when his mom threw a towel back at me and said, "Here, it can't be that bad." That was another big problem. His mom always had his back, and she believed he could never do anything wrong.

But for some reason, I continued to see him. It got to where he slapped me around often. But after every incident, he would always tell me he was sorry and that he wouldn't talk bad to me again, or do anything else to harm me. Then he would tell me how much he loved me and that he would kill himself if I ever left him. For a few days after every blow up, he would act sweet and caring, but then out of nowhere, he would blow up again. Whenever he would hit me, I would cry. That made him angrier and he would just hit me more.

> ## DESPITE EVERYTHING THAT HAD HAPPENED, I DECIDED TO HAVE SEX WITH NATE.

Despite everything that had happened, I decided to have sex with Nate. Maybe if I proved my love he wouldn't be so jealous and controlling. But I was wrong. He became even more controlling.

Then I became pregnant. My family kicked me out, and I moved in with Nate at his mother's house. Nate dropped out of school and got a low-paying job without insurance. I dropped out and found two part-time jobs. I always thought things would work out, and since I was going to have his baby, I thought that maybe he would eventually treat me better. I was dead wrong. Nate continued to beat me, spit on me, and call me names. He told me he'd kill me and the baby. He said he'd never pay child support. What was I thinking? He's telling me he'll kill me and the baby, and I think he loves me! What kind of love is that? But I couldn't see the truth in front of me.

Then something surprising began happening. I found myself growing closer to Christ and praying about the situation. Finally, one Sunday I walked to the front of the church and asked for prayer. I told them my situation and how I wanted out of my relationship with Nate. I said that I thought Nate would someday kill me and the baby.

Not long after I had asked for prayer, I made the decision to leave Nate and never go back. While Nate was at work and his mother was out, friends from church came and helped me move. I knew I only had a

NOT LONG AFTER I HAD ASKED FOR PRAYER, I MADE THE DECISION TO LEAVE NATE AND NEVER GO BACK.

short time to get everything of mine out before Nate or his mother returned. I was scared Nate would come home and kill us all, but I kept praying and packing. I wanted to get out as quickly as possible so I only took the most important things.

The church helped me find a place with some roommates. I got a job and went back to night school.

With the help of my friends and the church, I keep moving forward. And with God's help, my baby and I will be just fine.

Physical abuse is often called **domestic violence**. It's a crime committed by both genders, but statistically it's more often men committing the crime against women and children. Some reports indicate that a woman is physically abused every 15 seconds in America.

If it's not you, but you know someone who is being abused, here are some tips to help:

- Don't be judgmental.
- Offer your help and support.
- Realize it may be hard for the person to talk about things.
- The solution is not as easy as someone just following your advice.
- Encourage her (or him) any way you can.

—The National Council on Child Abuse and Family Violence
(www.nccafv.org)

UNLOCKING THE SECRET

When you've invested in a relationship that probably started out good with excitement for the future, it can be hard for you to believe that it could go so wrong. And to acknowledge that the person you love and chose to be with could really be an abuser is even harder still.

Abusers are great at telling you what you need to hear to keep you from leaving them. If you are in an abusive relationship, deep in your soul you know this. In public, people might consider him as the least likely person to be an abuser. He might be very popular. And that can be very confusing and cause you to doubt yourself. Abusers know when to act loving enough that you will begin to believe the person you fell in love with is back. But that person hasn't returned. Instead the abuser is waiting to come out literally punching. And that will be followed quickly by the heartfelt apology. The one you've heard many, many times. The one where he cries.

Emotional abuse always comes before violence. Abusers hook you emotionally, then build up to where they are okay with hurting you or convince themselves in the moment that you deserve it because of how they are feeling. Most physically abusive relationships start out initially with what may seem mild in the end (a push or a grab or a shove) and get more severe (a black eye, cuts, bruises, broken bones, trips to the emergency room, even death) over time. But hear this, *no abuse of any kind is okay!* Abusers aren't bad people, but they do bad things. They are hurt, angry, out-of-control people who act out their hurt on others. And if you are still with an abuser, chances are, you are really good at seeing the good in him and minimizing the bad, or having compassion for his hurt *but not your own.* You are not wrong for loving, but naive about your own ability to love someone out of abusing.

Here are the facts: Often you want the abuse to end, but you don't want the relationship to end. If the apology is truly heartfelt, he will understand why the two of you need help and should not see each other while each of you work through issues with a counselor. If he isn't willing to do this, he isn't willing to change because it doesn't bother him to hit you. Remember: Abusers never change (even if they want to change) without some type of professional intervention—and that means sharing your secret with an adult. You might think you can help him on your own, but you can't. And in a dating relationship you have no obligation to stay, no marital vows before God, and it isn't your job to fix him. Leaving is your best chance to save yourself and may have the greatest impact on the abuser finally getting help.

If you find yourself in a situation like Samantha's, the abuser might try to convince you that the abuse is your fault, that you are trapped, worthless, and maybe even insane. Or if only you committed more of yourself to him things would be different. Proving your love through greater devotion (or worse yet marrying him) will not make a difference. In fact it will make things worse once he feels he owns you. That's the way abusers keep you in their grasp. Get help now. Someone you trust can help you work through these issues and help you be safe.

There are no easy answers to physical abuse. You may be fearful and lack hope, but there is help available from a wide variety of resources including churches and community and government organizations. Two good resources are

- The National Council on Child Abuse and Family Violence, www.nccafv.org
- Making Waves, www.mwaves.org

For more services, turn to the Resources section that starts on page 217.

NO MORE SECRETS

If you are in an abusive situation, you might

- be afraid or embarrassed to let people know what's going on;

- be worried that others will overreact and want you to leave the relationship or think badly about you or your boyfriend;
- have fear for your safety and overall well-being, but still love him;
- feel like you have to stick it out because you have nowhere else to go or can't imagine emotionally letting go;
- avoid the issue so you don't upset him, and don't put yourself in any further danger.

But physical abuse puts you in a dangerous situation. Please know that it's okay to take this secret to another person. When you seek support, counsel, and prayer, other people can help you.

Think about your own situation. Then take a few minutes to answer the following questions, either here or in your private notebook.

I know I am physically abused, but I hide what's going on because

_____

_____

_____

_____

Even though some things are not in my control, some things are in my control. Things I can control include

_____

_____

_____

_____

How can others help you with the situation you are in?

_____

_____

_____

List one step you will take today to stop being hurt:

_____

_____

SECRET STRENGTH

"Even if I walk through a very dark valley, I will not be afraid, because you are with me. Your rod and your shepherd's staff comfort me."—PSALM 23:4

Someone has hurt me sexually.

*S*exual abuse can happen in several ways. If someone wants to touch you or asks you to touch them in areas that make you uncomfortable, when you don't want them to and it's clear you do not want it, this is sexual harassment. If someone pushes the issue and touches you in your "private parts," or if someone shows you his or her private parts and you don't want this person to (even if you are a little curious), it is sexual abuse.

Sexual abuse could involve incest or any unwanted oral sex, masturbation, or sexual intercourse. Sexual abuse is also being shown x-rated books, movies, or Internet porn sites when you don't want to see these, or being used in a pornographic production of any kind. For example, if a guy is your age and he doesn't respect your "no," or your body, or isn't absolutely sure you are a willing participant in wanting the sexual behavior, or if he convinces you to play along—he is taking advantage of you and this is a form of sexual abuse. If a person is older than you, more experienced than you, a family member, or a person in authority or has power over you and involves you in any kind of sexual behavior, sexual exposure, or sexual play—this is a form of molestation.

Abusers will make you feel that you had a part in initiating the abuse and will cause you to feel threatened if you expose them. Even if you think you were willing or couldn't say no, you were still being molested. And molestation *is always sexual abuse.*

If you have been sexually abused, or if it's still ongoing, talk to someone you trust about it. You do not have to be sexually abused. Seek help—even if you are no longer being sexually abused. Megan was sexually abused; you might relate to her story or know someone who would.

THE SECRET

Megan's Story

I am a homeschooled junior in high school and a Christian.

When I was three years old, something happened to me. Here's the short version: One day we were visiting some of my mom's family at my grandparents' house and one of my distant relatives, who was a teenager then, asked my mom if he could take me downstairs to play video games. My mom consented and we went to the basement. While we were there, he molested me.

As soon as we were in the car on the way home, I told my mom what had happened. Being so young, I didn't know that what happened was wrong, so it became my parents' burden to carry, and they were both furious. Apparently they tried to press charges and take action, but the police couldn't find any evidence except for the claims of a three-year-old kid, and they couldn't do anything about it.

Soon after the incident happened, my family moved away from the area and that relative—and for a long time the sexual abuse was not discussed.

I always had a vague memory of what had happened to me, but I hardly gave it any thought until the summer I turned 13. For some reason, one day everything clicked. I don't know why it never had before. I realized that if the memory I had was valid, I had been sexually abused, and the seemingly fun-loving family member was not the great guy I thought he was.

Since the abuse had happened ten years prior, I didn't fully trust this "memory," although it haunted me every day for an entire summer.

That summer I became very emotionally fragile and felt insecure. I felt like I was going crazy, thinking about the molestation constantly, wondering whether or not it had really happened. Previously, I decided I was going to forget about it, and if it did happen, I would live in ignorance and never let it bother me. But at some point during that summer, I came to the conclusion that mental peace would not be possible unless I at least asked someone about it. I knew that my mother was the right person to ask.

I FELT LIKE I WAS GOING CRAZY, THINKING ABOUT THE MOLESTATION CONSTANTLY, WONDERING WHETHER OR NOT IT HAD REALLY HAPPENED.

Although I came to that decision on my own, I stalled for the rest of the summer, and kept going back and forth in my mind about wanting to know or not and how to bring it up. The prospect of asking my mother this question about a relative was embarrassing and horrifying. But I knew I had to get this secret out somehow, because it was suffocating me. So I first told one of my good friends. Then I told a couple more friends, hoping they would be able to enlighten me on how to handle my situation. They were kind and caring, but all felt that the best solution was to ask my mother about what had happened.

One day in the car on our way to pick my sister up from a friend's house, I found myself alone with my mom. I knew this was a "now or never" moment. I kept looking out the window. There was a huge knot in my stomach. I began to cry. "Mom?" I asked feebly. After a few minutes of hesitation and my mom asking what was wrong, I stammered out the question. "Did . . . something . . . bad . . . happen to me when I was little?"

She knew what I meant. Her answer was yes, and I began to sob.

God knew what he was doing by giving me the courage to ask the question on that particular day, because my sister's friend's mom, who was also one of my mom's best friends and a great friend of our family, had been through a similar situation. While my sister and her friend stayed down the hall, my mom and I talked to her friend. In relating to her, I didn't feel so alone and that was a huge comfort—but things inside of me didn't change right away.

Over that fall and winter I sunk into a pit of depression that felt worse than ever before. When I got out of bed in the morning, it was on my mind. When I did laundry, it was on my mind. For a while I used food to push away the feelings. I could escape some of my pain when I was with my boyfriend, but he became an idol in my life. I began thinking about death a lot and doing small things to hurt myself. I felt like I was trapped inside my head all the time. I felt like I was going crazy.

I went into depression, numbness, and denial. But the end result was bitterness and hatred. I couldn't stand the sight of this relative, and I fantasized about hurting him. But beyond kicking the tires on his truck, I never followed through. But in my heart, I murdered him again and again.

> *I WENT INTO DEPRESSION, NUMBNESS, AND DENIAL. BUT THE END RESULT WAS BITTERNESS AND HATRED.*

I felt really bad about myself and turned my anger toward God, deciding that I was not a Christian anymore. My friend noticed a change in me and began praying for me. She asked me why I didn't raise my arms in worship anymore, or why I didn't take communion, and I would tell her "I didn't feel like it," or that "I was tired," which were both true.

I got further and further away from God until right after New Year's. My boyfriend and I had just broken up, which did not help my depression at all. I had started going to a new youth group, and they were all so excited about God. During worship the teenage guys would get into it, closing their eyes, which I had never seen before. The guys I had been around were usually more reserved and "cool" about the way they worshiped. This sounds quite cliché, but when I was around my new friends, I felt like something was missing in my life. I knew what it was. God had never stopped calling me back to himself. I simply didn't let myself hear him because of my hurt. But being around people who were so obviously in love with God helped me draw near to him again.

Still, I was stubborn and did not let myself "give in." At that point in my life, I might have even been willing to give myself away physically. Thank God I never did. I had begun to see my emotional distance as strength, and this included emotional distance from God.

My mom knew something was wrong with me, and while she didn't try to force me to love God, she did make me sit with our family while she read out loud to us. She read Joni, by Joni Eareckson Tada, an autobiography about how she broke her neck in a diving accident and became paralyzed for life at the age of 17. Her book deals with the ups and downs she experienced in her spiritual walk with God because of her accident and her bitterness over what had happened to her. In her book she expounds over and over again about the bitterness she dealt with at not being able to do all the little things she used to take for granted. I could relate to what she was feeling so well, not to her paralysis, but to the bitterness she was talking about. After each chapter my mom read, the eloquence with which Joni told her story drew me in and made me feel as if I had been paralyzed too.

Joni told how she had returned to God, and I thought that was amazing. I felt guilty after reading her story each night, thinking that I could walk and run and swim and do almost anything that I physically wanted to do, but yet I remained bitter toward God because of the abuse; but Joni, who was destined to spend her life in a wheelchair, was able to overcome her bitterness and allow God to become her joy and strength. I wanted that.

My new youth group and reading Joni's story were the two main things that God used to draw me back to himself. One night while I was lying in bed hoping fiercely that I would not die in my sleep, a fear I had since I decided *that I was not a Christian, I suddenly realized, "I do not have to live like this anymore."*

For a few moments, the emotional disengagement that I felt would make me stronger kept me from talking to God. I lay there with the covers wrapped tightly around me and whispered this prayer, "God, give me the strength to surrender, because I don't want to." After that, I prayed to him freely and woke my sister up with sobs of joy. I finally felt free.

I talked to my mom and sister until late that night, and fell asleep feeling peace for the first time in a long time. At the moment I rededicated my life to God, I knew that forgiving my abuser would be an important step in setting me free to walk unhindered with Christ.

Once I gave Christ complete control, forgiveness was much easier than I thought it would be.

UNLOCKING THE SECRET

Megan is not alone. If you have been a victim of sexual abuse or child molestation, God understands how you feel and what you are going through. He wants you to feel safe and secure again, and he wants you to be able to trust that he will somehow work this painful situation out for good.

If you were a young child when this happened to you, you may not completely remember it or understand it until later. It may take you awhile to come to grips with what happened. It is normal to have questions and to become upset when you are a victim of someone else's abuse.

Unfortunately, there is wickedness and evil in this world and in the hearts of people, even God's people. We all have the same ability to choose evil or to make wrong choices, just as we do to choose good and to make right choices. We all are responsible for our own actions or reactions, our own body, and our own choices. However, as children and then adolescents, your choices are more limited and controlled by the adults in your life. You probably felt or still feel trapped in the pain of abuse. And even though someone else hurt you by crossing your sexual and body boundaries, you have to be the one to ask for and be willing to seek the help you need.

God understands your pain. He's there in the times when you feel alone, afraid, ashamed, and embarrassed. He did not want you to be abused. He saw what happened and his heart was broken by the evil choice your abuser made. He wants to help you heal, ease your hurts, and help you move through it to a place where the abuse no longer defines you, where you can be free—not to condone your abuser's actions, but to release them to God's vengeance and not yours. This is the freedom of forgiving yourself and others.

Like Megan, you can learn to heal by using these four forgiveness points.

1. Reveal to God, yourself, and others you trust what happened to you and how it has hurt you.

Care about yourself enough to let God and others into your painful secrets. Feel the feelings and sit with the anger, hurt, or shame in the presence of caring family, friends, and/or a counselor. Refuse to believe the lies of your abuser. Know that you are not a bad or lesser person because you were abused. God doesn't love people who weren't abused more than you. God loves you. He cares about your life. He understands how hard it is for you to forget a wrong committed against you. He wants what's best for you. In Jeremiah 29:11 it says, "'I say this because I know what I am planning for you,' says the Lord. 'I have good plans for you, not plans to hurt you. I will give you hope and a good future.'" Forgive yourself.

2. Forgiveness is a process, not something that happens all at once.

People think that forgiveness is just waking up and having warm, fuzzy feelings toward someone who has hurt them. It's not like that. Forgiveness is a choice and a process like anything else. It's natural to want to hold a grudge and let it fester inside you like an infected wound. Make a list of those who have hurt you.

- The abuser—for selfishly using you
- Parents and friends—for not knowing or not believing you
- God—for not stopping the abuse from happening
- Yourself—for not knowing what to do
- Your body—for responding with physical sensations

You have to say, "Today, I choose to forgive," or "Today, I choose to not let this person continue to hurt me by monopolizing my thoughts and feelings"—just for today and not all at once. You don't need to rush the timing. Resolve to begin considering forgiveness on this day or when you feel ready. Then make that resolution every day—and ask God to help you keep it. Remember: Forgiveness is for your freedom; God will deal with the other person in his way and in his time. Forgive God.

3. There are no excuses for abuse.

Do not try to rationalize what a person did to you. Compassion is good for understanding, and understanding can ease pain, but it does not excuse actions. Depending on your situation, "walking in someone else's moccasins" can be a helpful aid in the process of forgiving someone, or it can be a frustration that only feeds a grudge. A wrong is a wrong no matter why it happened. You may never know why the person hurt you, but what you must do in situations like this is to resolve to be free from the hurt controlling the rest of your life. You do this by learning to forgive and basing forgiveness on your actions and not theirs.

- No matter if they apologize or if they don't apologize.
- No matter if they admit what they did or don't ever admit it.
- No matter if they're angry and blame you or have no reaction at all.
- No matter if they change or if they don't change.
- No matter if they're wrong.

No matter what . . . forgive their wrongs.

4. The best reason to forgive is for you.

Once you forgive someone, you are no longer tied to that person in any way. You are free of him or her and his or her mistake. Whatever the person did is no longer your burden or shame to carry. There's an old saying, "Bitterness is like drinking poison and waiting for someone else to die." Gosh, if this worked, wouldn't we all try it, at least once, to have someone pay for the selfish, awful thing he or she did to us. When it comes to unforgivingness, this is very true, and a great thing to remember. You may feel powerful by holding a grudge, but in reality—by your own hatred—you are tying yourself to them. Examine what you are still wanting to hold on to or what you think you need from them. Realize how much you are giving them power over you by holding on to your anger, hurt, bitterness, and unforgivingness. Don't let them have that power; free yourself. Forgive others.

NO MORE SECRETS

If you are a victim of a sexual crime, it is natural for you to feel

- Anger
- Embarrassment
- Shame
- Frustration
- Pain

If your secret is that you were sexually abused, let's do some work in this area right now. Take some time to write your answers, either here or in your private notebook.

I know I was sexually abused. It happened when I was about age _____ . Here's what happened:

_____

_____

_____

The primary emotion I feel today when I look at that experience is

_____

_____

Some ways I will seek help in this area are

_____

_____

My prayer is
(Write a forgiveness prayer.)

_____

_____

_____

_____

_____

_____

Amen.

SECRET STRENGTH

"Do not be bitter or angry or mad. Never shout angrily or say things to hurt others. Never do anything evil. Be kind and loving to each other, and forgive each other just as God forgave you in Christ."—EPHESIANS 4:31–32

I'm pregnant.

*i*n the throes of passion, a girl and a guy aren't thinking about being called mom and dad—they are thinking about their feelings in the moment, almost as if nothing else exists. And even if they have the forethought to use contraception, it is never 100 percent effective. Girls still get pregnant. And when they do, it is often the girl's lifestyle and education that are most affected. As you'll see in the following stories, the guy may or may not take responsibility, or stay in the girl's or baby's life.

THE SECRET

Renee's Story

I was a rebellious teenager, and I thought I knew everything. When I was 15, I dropped out of school, ran away from home, hung around the wrong crowd, and did a lot of things that were not good for me.

At 16, I found out I was going to have a baby. I'll never forget that day. I was surprised, confused, and not sure what to do. I went back to my boyfriend, not knowing how he would react to the news. But he was supportive of me. Later I learned I was having two babies. Twins!

I remember thinking I needed to return to school. And then I thought, How am I going to finish high school with two babies on the way? *But I was deter-mined to go back to high school and graduate.*

As my belly grew, my boyfriend and I began to wonder if we were ready to stay together and raise a family, or if we should ask our parents for help. But we were too embarrassed to contact them.

I kept busy working, got married to my babies' father, and studied every chance I got so that I could graduate from high school. He got into a local program that helped him learn a trade, so he could get a better job. It was a lot of hard work, but God gave us the strength, determination, and abilities to succeed. His grace allowed us to overcome things that seemed impossible to me. Now I am very proud of the fact that I am a good mother. And I thank God each and every day.

Natalie's Story

When I started dating Kaden, I was pretty sure we would have sex. Kaden had sex with two girls before he dated me. I know you're not supposed to have sex before you marry, but I wondered what sex would be like. I was only 15, but I had seen it so many times in movies I wasn't scared. I just wanted to be close to Kaden.

We had sex a lot for maybe three months before we broke up. It feels a bit embarrassing saying this, but Kaden didn't always use a condom when we had sex, and I didn't insist he use one. He said he didn't like the way it felt.

About a month after we broke up, I missed my period. I had been late before and was never really that regular so it didn't concern me much. But then my body started feeling weird, and I started throwing up in the morning. I bought a home pregnancy test and the line showed blue. Now what was I supposed to do?

> ABOUT A MONTH AFTER WE BROKE UP, I MISSED MY PERIOD.

I absolutely couldn't tell my parents. My mom has never been that stable anyway, and my dad was a minister—so he would be embarrassed and I thought that maybe he could lose his job (which later I found out was not true). I knew it was wrong, but to make a long story short, Kaden gave me the money to go to a clinic to get the "problem" taken care of.

On the way in there were picketers outside. I live in a state where you don't have to notify your parents if you're under 18. Afterward I joined the rest of the girls in the lobby drinking orange juice and eating cookies.

I feel a lot of shame and guilt for what I did. And I'm trying to get my life right with God, but it's just so hard. I know what I did was wrong. I still haven't told my parents. I doubt if I ever will. Sometimes I wake up in the middle of the night and wonder who that baby could have become.

No matter what you might be going through, remember that God knows you and he loves you. He understands your

- thoughts,
- feelings,
- questions,
- fears,
- hopes, and
- desires.

Trust him. Talk to him. He promises he'll be there for you.

UNLOCKING THE SECRET

It might be easier not to talk about teen pregnancy, but it happens. It can be devastating for a young woman who's not married to find out she's pregnant. A child is a wonderful thing, but having a baby certainly complicates life. Renee beat the odds. She got married and finished high school. But many young mothers don't do either of those things. And many young fathers run from the responsibility. It's not always best to marry someone just because of pregnancy. But facing the reality of your situation and letting others help you is the best chance for good to come out of your circumstances. A good friend of mine always says, "Do the next right thing." When he was young, he paid for an abortion for a girl he got pregnant; now a Christian ministry leader, he speaks throughout the country at crisis pregnancy centers to help young women not go through the pain he felt. By reaching out and letting people know his secret, he has turned his mistake into giving others hope.

There is never a more fertile time than in your teens and twenties to get pregnant, due to the wider window of opportunity that young women's bodies allow. In your thirties that window starts closing and by your midforties it is almost impossible.

Natalie's story is sadder. She chose to take matters into her own hands and keep her situation secret. She chose to have an abortion even though she believed what she was doing was wrong. Her fear of her parents' disappointment and embarrassment in their position kept her from including them in a huge life decision. She'll never know if they would have formed a strong support network to rally around her through the difficult decisions or not. Instead, Natalie tried to simplify her life by not having a baby.

But some mistakes can't be as easily erased as we think, and there can be lingering consequences to our choices long after they are made. Each choice Natalie made had a consequence that affected her life.

- The choice to glamorize sex, thinking she would be closer to her boy-friend, only to break up a month later.
- The choice to go against what she knew to be right by having sex outside of marriage instead of delaying gratification and waiting for God's timing.
- The choice to *not* use protection because it was bothersome, which resulted in her becoming pregnant.

Natalie's choice to hide her secret and deal with it on her own has already caused her guilt. What she doesn't realize is that her abortion didn't end with her baby's life, but will continue to cause her emotional pain for years to come unless she chooses to seek help. In making choices against her beliefs, her life and faith have suffered.

If you're pregnant (or know a teen who is), know that God still loves you and has a plan for your life. He can help you with whatever you are going through. He can bring about good in all things. The act of getting pregnant was a mistake, but once you've conceived, your baby is no mistake. If you're facing a situation like Renee's or Natalie's, God can help you. He knows that you might be feeling scared, afraid, and uneasy about what you are going through, but he will always be there for you.

Several ministries and Christian organizations can help. There are Christian crisis pregnancy centers in almost every large city throughout the nation, with people who want to help you walk through dealing with your unexpected pregnancy. There are support groups for before and after you have your baby, or adoption help (if that's right for you). And if you couldn't wait and took matters into your own hands and had an abortion, there are much-needed support groups for you as well. Don't deny, avoid, or suffer alone; learn from your situation and get help to move through it.

Mercy Ministries of America (www.mercyministries.org) helps young women facing a variety of difficult circumstances, such as unplanned pregnancy. Another good organization is Birthright International (www.Birthright.com). BI's 24-hour free hotline is 1-866-576-2764. For more suggestions, turn to the Resources section that starts on page 217.

NO MORE SECRETS

If your secret is pregnancy, please get help right away. Tell someone you can trust, who can help you work through this difficult time. Regardless of what you decide to do, you need a support network that includes adults.

To help you take the first steps, take a few minutes to answer the following questions, either here or in your private notebook.

Write down what you would like God to know about how you are feeling right now.

_____

_____

_____

_____

Name three ways you can help yourself.

_____

_____

_____

How can others help you?

_____

_____

_____

What will you say when you ask them for that help?

_____

_____

_____

In what ways will you ask God to help and protect you?

_____

_____

_____

My prayer is

God,
You know me. Please forgive me for my mistakes. Help me to
trust you even though I don't know what to do. Please show me
what to do and where to go for help.
Amen.

SECRET STRENGTH

"Since we have been made right with God by our faith,
we have peace with God. This happened through our
Lord Jesus Christ, who through our faith has brought us
into that blessing of God's grace that we now enjoy. And
we are happy because of the hope we have of sharing
God's glory. We also have joy with our troubles, because
we know that these troubles produce patience. And
patience produces character, and character produces
hope. And this hope will never disappoint us, because
God has poured out his love to fill our hearts. He gave us
his love through the Holy Spirit, whom God has given to
us."—ROMANS 5:1–5

I have no idea what I want to do in life.

*g*uess what? If you're not sure what you want to do in life, you're not alone. But here's the good news: You can change your mind, and with God's help you can change careers at any age. Vanessa trusted God to help her decide on her goals.

THE SECRET

Vanessa's Story

I think my brother was born knowing that he wanted to be a teacher. And my little sister's musical talents were obvious. She was working in musicals by the time she was five. But not me. I've never known what I wanted to do. My parents put me in class after class after class. I learned to twirl, to dance, to program computers. I've built stage sets and volunteered at the local library and hospital. I felt like my parents were disappointed in me, although they never said so. The only thing I was even remotely good at was art. I could draw just about anything, but that's not really a career.

I began to get impatient and asked God if he was ever going to show me what I'm suppose to do—because I had no clue.

Then one day I went to an astronomy class at the local museum. I liked it okay. But I really liked the guy sitting next to me, Raymond. He was fun to be with, and every chance he got he was there studying the stars. So when they offered another class, I took it. My parents were so excited. They saw my eagerness to get to the class. They thought I'd found a career path I was passionate about, and I didn't want to disappoint them. So they kept signing me up for more classes, and I just kept going.

I started helping Raymond by drawing some of his star maps. And then some of the museum's staff asked me to help them create some posters. Then one day the staff asked me if I'd like to try and create a poster for their new exhibit. I did and they liked it enough to reproduce it.

Things just kept going along . . . I kept attending astronomy classes, Raymond and I started dating, and other groups started asking me to create art for their projects. Everything was fine—until it came time to start looking at colleges. My parents wanted me to attend a college with a strong astronomy department. But I really didn't want to go into astronomy; I just didn't know how to tell them.

Then one day the marketing director of the museum came in to talk to me. She'd been admiring my art and asked me if I'd like to study art. She said that there were different degrees in art majors, and if I would like, she'd recommend me for a scholarship to the college she attended. I said yes, and she helped me fill out the paperwork.

I didn't tell my parents, but they did find out when the college sent the scholarship package. My dad brought it in and asked me to open it. Before I did, I told them my secret. Their reaction stunned me. They gave me a family hug. They weren't disappointed in me; they just were being supportive. If I didn't want to study astronomy, that was okay.

I'm still not sure exactly what I want to do, but for now I'd like to study art. I know that God designed my talents and my gifts. He always surpasses our greatest expectations. God has started opening doors for me that are giving me even greater opportunities to demonstrate my talent. I'm not sure how

*God will use me and the talent he gave me for his work, but I know firsthand
that his plan is always best.*

UNLOCKING THE SECRET

God chose to reveal Vanessa's plan for her in his own time,
in ways that far exceeded her expectations. We often limit God to
the one or two options we see. We think there is only "Plan A" or
"Plan B," but most of the time God has a "Plan C" that we've never
thought of with an even greater plan and purpose for our lives.

Sometimes young women know early on their passions and
talents. As with Vanessa, that's not always the case. Sometimes it
takes awhile for a passion or talent to be recognized. You don't need
to worry about having it all figured out. This is a time to be open to
opportunities that God puts into your
life. For most people what they thought
they wanted to be or started out doing
doesn't look anything like what they
end up doing. And if you are a person
who is interested in growing—even if
you do know what you want to do—
hopefully it will evolve and change as you grow. The important
thing is to trust God to help guide you to your goals.

> *SOMETIMES IT
> TAKES AWHILE
> FOR A PASSION
> OR TALENT TO BE
> RECOGNIZED.*

For me, I never imagined I'd be a radio co-host. It wasn't
ever even on my screen. I always had two passions, well maybe
three—art and psychology, and being a Christian. So I attended
a Christian university and set out to accomplish both. Growing
up, I always enjoyed art and was a good listener who had a heart
for people's struggles. Eventually being a psychologist over an
artist won out. So now I wear bright colors, do creative things at

home, use art therapy with groups, and get to help people through Christian ministry over the airways or in my office one-on-one. In high school, I could have never picked a career I love more. But one step at a time, and being open to what God can do, he combined the talents and desires he gave me into what I do today.

Right now, you might be confused as to your goals. You might be eager to get out of school and start your career. But take some time to investigate your career options. Think about what you enjoy doing. What are you good at doing? Do you like computer programming? Playing video games? Someone has to create, design, build, oversee, market—everything. Maybe your skill is with people. Would you like to be an ambassador? A teacher? A hair stylist? A lawyer? Maybe like Vanessa your hobby will become your career goal. Do you like to shop? Maybe your career is in fashion as a buyer or designer. Take advantage of career and personality tests through your school. Talk with your parents and friends about your skills. They might be seeing a gift you haven't noticed. Be open to a combination of things that may involve, not only career goals, but also family, relationship, and lifestyle goals.

Ultimately, God's plan involved Vanessa's talents, gifts, and desires combined with his ultimate purpose for her life. God already knew the desires of her heart before she asked him for anything. He also took the time to prepare her for what he had in store for her to do. At times, we might feel like Vanessa did—lacking the patience to see what God is going to do, so we begin to question him.

But I believe that whatever route he takes us, we have to trust that he knows what is best for us. God is always behind the scenes working things out for us.

Ask God to do his work in your life and to bless your endeavors. Then as you see his plan for your life unfold, you will be amazed at the work he is accomplishing in you and through you.

As you seek him, God will reveal the best path for you. Ephesians 1:10–12 says, "His goal was to carry out his plan, when the right time came, that all things in heaven and on earth would be joined together in Christ as the head. In Christ we were chosen to be God's people, because from the very beginning God had decided this in keeping with his plan. And he is the One who makes everything agree with what he decides and wants. We are the first people who hoped in Christ, and we were chosen so that we would bring praise to God's glory."

We can stick to God's plan for our lives by

- asking him to guide us,
- praying for wisdom,
- seeking him in all aspects of our lives,
- acknowledging he has a plan and a purpose,
- thanking him for what he has done for us,
- talking to wise people, and
- reading his Word.

NO MORE SECRETS

If your secret is that you have no idea what to do in life, you're not alone. But God knows his plans for you. Let's do some work in this area. Take a few minutes to answer the following questions, either here or in your private notebook.

What are your passions in life?

_____

_____

What are your hobbies?

_____

What are you really good at?

_____

What would your family and friends say are your talents?

_____

_____

In five years, what would you like to be doing?

_____

_____

How can we know for sure that God has a plan for us?

_____

_____

What does God's plan for your life look like right now? (Describe how you see it.)

_____

_____

What are some of the things that might be keeping you from discovering God's plan for your life?

_____

_____

What can help you understand the difference between God's plan for your life versus your own plan?

_____

_____

Name some of the ways your life is bringing glory to God.

_____

_____

What are three things that you can do to prepare for what God has in store for your life?

_____

_____

SECRET STRENGTH

"Each of you has received a gift to use to serve others. Be good servants of God's various gifts of grace."
—1 PETER 4:10

YOU'VE TOLD YOUR SECRET— NOW WHAT HAPPENS?

*b*y telling someone your secret, your goal is to seek help, find a solution, and step into a secret-free life. You have taken an important step toward a secret-free life. Regardless of the reaction of the person you tell, you might feel some relief that the secret is out.

What happens after you've told your secret will depend on the nature of your secret. For example, if your secret is that you have an eating disorder, the next steps might be to see a physician and a therapist. On the other hand, if your secret is more that you have a hard time saying no to your friends, the next step might be advice from your parents or a counselor.

. . . .

"The teaching of a wise person gives life. It is like a
fountain that can save people from death."
—PROVERBS 13:14

. . . .

Tell, then listen!

By telling someone your secret, you are sharing part of your inner self with another person. You are creating an opportunity for you both to feel connected and loved and to get the help you need. At first the person's feedback may be hard to hear, but stop and listen. Remember: Keeping your secret was not getting you anywhere. Receiving difficult truth, honest love, acceptance, and guidance from caring people is all part of the healing process God intended. When others give us time to feel heard and to share our hurts, mistakes, and secrets, it strengthens us and lifts our spirit. It helps to move us out of aloneness and into healing solutions. Tell your secret, listen to what the person you trust says—even if it's not what you want to hear—and consider what he or she has said. Then step into the relief of a secret-free life.

- If you tend to listen with your body twisted up like a pretzel, physically unwrap your body. Uncross your arms and legs.
- Maintain eye contact with the speaker.
- Focus on what the speaker is saying.
- When you speak, speak quietly but loudly enough for the adult to hear you.
- Ask questions.

The follow-through . . .

One of the hardest but most important things to do after revealing a secret is the follow-through. Consider this step your ticket to living secret free. The follow-through might include . . .

- consequences, such as having to pay off a speeding ticket or being grounded for being tattooed without your parents' permission, or
- a lifelong change, such as avoiding drugs and alcohol

Remember: Harmful secrets only thrive if we let them. If later you feel like you are being tempted to keep a harmful secret, tell someone you trust. Take some time to talk with God about your problem.

One step at a time.
This is the fifth step to living a secret-free life. Write down your thoughts in the space here or in your private notebook.

My follow-through involves

_____

_____

_____

My prayer is

_____

_____

_____

_____

Amen.

I smoke, I do drugs, I get drunk (or I'm tempted to).

harmful substances are all around us. They're a part of our culture. You may feel that you are constantly being tempted to experiment with smoking, drinking, or drugs. You are not alone. Some give into the temptation; others do not. What makes the difference?

THE SECRET

Riley's Story

In junior high school, I struggled with alcohol and drug abuse. There are many reasons why, but the first reason is definitely popularity. Junior high is filled with lots of pressures—and I think I felt them all. My parents divorced. I wanted to be more like my older sister. I wanted to be popular. I wanted to fit in. As the pressures built, I started smoking and soon I was drinking.

Many times I smoked and drank with my older sister. I really wanted a connection with her, especially after my mom left. I quickly learned that being like my sister made her want me around more. But I wasn't paying attention to who she really was and what she was doing. Following in her footsteps of bad behavior only led me down the path to trouble. I began drinking more and started using drugs. While I was using, I found that I could forget about the problems that caused me stress. This lasted only a short time because lying and hiding my using caused stress on top of the other stress in my life.

Once I was caught and everyone knew about my addictions, there was a family intervention. I agreed to attend a small recovery group at my church called "Life Hurts, GOD HEALS." This group made such a difference in my life. It helped me become sober. It helped me to understand that the choices my sister was making were not good examples for my life. I can love her without following her example. Now I learn from her mistakes, rather than make the same ones. It helped me to also realize that I am not the only one who has problems. Most of all, it helped me understand God's love for me, and how he forgives and heals. I learned that there is no one God cannot heal and no mistake he cannot forgive. God has made my life much easier.

G.O.D.H.E.A.L.S.

Step 1: Get Help

Step 2: Open Your Heart

Step 3: Depend on Christ

Step 4: Hear and Speak

Step 5: Embrace God's Way

Step 6: Ask for Forgiveness

Step 7: Live for God

Step 8: Support Others

—From *Life Hurts, God Heals*, by Megan Hutchinson and Doug Fields (www.simplyyouthministry.com)

UNLOCKING THE SECRET

Riley knows she made a series of bad decisions. Using drugs and alcohol caused her unnecessary pain and trouble. Her addictions were an attempt to alleviate the pain she felt from several things including peer pressure, stress, family problems, and her parents' divorce. When Riley's secret was discovered, she got the help she needed.

The particular program Riley attended is open to students in sixth through twelfth grades, and is based on an eight-step program centered on the acronym G.O.D.H.E.A.L.S. (For more information, see the box on page 177.)

Some helpful truths on avoiding drugs and alcohol:

- Not everyone is doing it.
- You can beat temptation.
- The wrong crowd is not the crowd for you.
- The wrong places are not the places to go.
- Don't give in to the lie that you will feel more accepted.
- Don't think it will help you be cool or build your self-confidence.

Some common signs of a drug or alcohol problem:

- Mood and Personality changes
- Drop in grades
- Red eyes
- Tired, sleep changes—getting too much or too little
- Absence from school
- Discipline problems
- Irresponsible behavior
- Breaking the rules

- Starting arguments with family members and friends
- Changing friends, withdrawing from family

If you find yourself in a situation like Riley's, help is always available. Contact a church in your area for local programs that can provide you with the support and help you need, and turn to the Resources section that starts on page 217 for more options.

Partying might seem like the thing to do because all your friends are doing it, or because it looks fun. But it can be costly. Your friends or people you hang with might give you the impression that smoking, drinking, and drugs are the thing to do, but the high is always short-lived. Staying away from it can save you a lot of trouble. There are many alternatives where you can have a fun, clean, and safe time without harmful substances. Ask God to help you choose the right friends and to help you make healthy and positive choices.

Who is an alcoholic?

All alcoholics start as innocent drinkers who—often in their teens—just want to feel more comfortable socially. No one sets out to be an alcoholic or a drug addict. Some people drink alcoholically from their first drink—meaning that they like the feeling so much that they keep drinking until drunk. Others may like the initial feeling—but they stop when they start to feel too tipsy or out of control. Many teens can have a bad experience where they drink too much, too fast, or on an empty stomach and get sick and vomit or pass out. This is a huge warning sign, and most only have to experience that once to never do it again. But those who either don't learn from bad experiences and continue to repeat them, or who seem to be able to "handle" drinking beyond what others can drink without getting sick are the people with the potential to develop alcoholism or other addictions.

If there are alcoholics and/or addicts in your family, like a grandparent, parent, or uncle, you need to be aware of how addictions run in families—and know that you may be more susceptible. Some people can hide their drinking problem for a long time, but untreated it will catch up with them.

An alcoholic becomes first emotionally and then physically addicted to alcohol to the point she can't function normally without it. There is no one who would choose this kind of bondage for the outcome of her life. Most think, *It could never happen to me*, especially when they are young. But ask any alcoholic after a lifetime of causing hurt and pain for herself and others and she will tell you she wishes she had not started drinking.

Drug addictions usually occur more rapidly than alcoholism. Some drugs like crack, cocaine, or meth can hook you from your first use. Tragically, death can also occur from one bad episode. "Rolling," where kids take a handful of different prescription meds from parents' medicine cabinets and try out different unknown meds to see what will happen, can be lethal. Doctors take great care in being aware of drug interactions that may be problematic when used together. Pot is still the most widely used drug and many teens feel it won't harm them since it also has usefulness in medicine as with cancer patients. But just remember, life can be about trade-offs and perspective: If you are dying from cancer, you are less worried about an addiction.

Drug addiction is not about the substance you are using (as many addicts have a preferred drug and the effects vary). Drug addiction is about repeated use of any substance that causes a decline in lifestyle and attitude and removes God from the center of your life and puts the drug in his place.

Coping with a parent or a friend who has an addiction to alcohol isn't easy. You may feel unloved, lonely, alone, helpless. Did you know, it's normal to feel that way?

According to the National Council on Alcoholism and Drug Dependence (NCADD—www.ncadd.org), there are nearly 14 million Americans who are considered problem drinkers, including 8 million who have alcoholism. Some 76 million people are exposed to alcoholism within their families.

NO MORE SECRETS

If your secret is use of a harmful substance, let's do some work in this area right now. Take a few minutes to answer the following questions, either here or in your private notebook.

Have you ever felt pressure to try drugs or alcohol when with friends who use? If so, how did you respond and what did you do?

If you are currently struggling with drugs or alcohol, describe what you're going through.

_____

_____

If this is your secret or a friend's secret, list sources you could go to for help.

_____

_____

Name four positive things you can choose to do on a Friday or Saturday night to avoid being pressured to use drugs or alcohol.

_____   _____

_____   _____

SECRET STRENGTH

"In the same way, you should see yourselves as being dead to the power of sin and alive with God through Christ Jesus. So, do not let sin control your life here on earth so that you do what your sinful self wants to do. Do not offer the parts of your body to serve sin, as things to be used in doing evil. Instead, offer yourselves to God as people who have died and now live. Offer the parts of your body to God to be used in doing good. Sin will not be your master, because you are not under law but under God's grace."—ROMANS 6:11–14

I have a hard time saying no to my friends

(even when I don't want to say yes).

have you ever felt like a friend was trying to get you to do something you didn't want to do? Peer pressure can take a lot of forms. A young woman named Kelley talked about the peer pressure of wanting to go along with the group, but knowing it's the wrong thing to do.

THE SECRET

Kelley's Story

I wanted to fit in with the other girls, but I always felt like somehow I was the outsider. Then this group of four girls started inviting me to go around with them. I tried to do what they did, but sometimes it didn't make me feel really good about myself. Like once the leader, Tina, was so mean to this one girl that the girl left crying. And Tina never studied. Instead she cheated off Jennifer, Frankie, or my tests and homework. But I liked feeling as if I belonged, so I played along.

For a long time, Tina had been talking about all of us getting tattoos and piercings—but we'd never done it. Then one day we were bored. Tina started talking about tattoos again. How cool they were and how she knew where there was a tattoo shop. We decided we'd do it. It would be an adventure.

By the time we got to the tattoo shop, I was getting queasy. I knew my parents would be mad if they found out, and I knew I didn't want to be poked by needles. Tina and Sue had run up to look at the tattoo styles pasted on the window, but I stood away from the shop. I knew it would mean being an outsider again, but I said a little prayer and then looked at the group and said I'd changed my mind. To my surprise, Jennifer and Frankie stood next to me and said they'd changed their minds too.

Then Tina got mean. She asked how we'd get home because she'd driven. I said my dad said no matter where I was or what I'd done, if I needed him to come pick me up, he would. I called him, and he took Jennifer, Frankie, and me home. Sue stayed with Tina. My dad didn't yell or anything; he just said we'd made a good decision, and he never mentioned it again.

What surprised me most is that when I said something, Jennifer and Frankie stepped forward too. Jennifer, Frankie, and I have become true friends. It turns out, we have a lot in common. When we started trusting each other enough to tell our secrets, we learned we'd all felt like outsiders. It made us wonder how many times each of us did the wrong thing, when if we'd done the right thing, some of the group might have joined us.

Parents of teenagers identified peer pressure as the biggest challenge faced by 13- to 18-year-olds.

—Good News Holdings telephone survey conducted by the Barna Research Group, 2006

"My friends and I were running late for a concert. I was driving. They kept saying go faster, go faster. Finally, Tam said even if the police stopped us we wouldn't get a ticket. She was right. The officer didn't give them a ticket. He gave it to me! I had to work to pay off the ticket, and no one offered to help. My parents also took away my driving privileges for a month!"—Erica

UNLOCKING THE SECRET

No matter what your age, peer pressure can be a big concern. Sometimes you receive pressure from your peers without even realizing it. They expect you to act in certain ways or do certain things that you don't feel comfortable with. Peer pressure pressures you to have to be cool or fit in or be accepted.

You might be like Kelley and want to fit in with a group, but if a group is pressuring you to do something you know is wrong, take time to step away and think about the consequences of your actions. More often than not, you are not the only one in the group who is feeling pressure to do the wrong thing, and by choosing to do the right thing your true friends will step forward.

It is especially hard to say no to others when you fear their rejection. No one likes to feel rejected, and some people learn to become people pleasers as a way to avoid rejection at all costs. The problem with this way of interacting is that over time the more you "people please" the more you give up *you*. In other words, you end up rejecting yourself and who God made you to be. You give up developing your own opinions, your own sense of style, and your own interests when you allow your fear of rejection to take over. Relationships really are about give and take, and if you are the one doing all the giving to a taker, your friendship is off balance. Sometimes it's helpful to compromise or do something pleasing for a friend, and other times it's right for you to speak up and state what you think. There are no guarantees that someone will always like you. If you never say no and always try to please as a way of keeping people close, you might find that they lose interest in you because you have made yourself an agreeable non-person. Ever feel invisible? Never saying no is the best way to get there.

Romans 12:2 offers some wise words concerning peer pressure: "Do not be shaped by this world; instead be changed within by a new way of thinking. Then you will be able to decide what God wants for you; you will know what is good and pleasing to him and what is perfect."

If you seek God in all things, even in light of peer pressure, he will make things clear for you. He will show you what he has in store for you. It's comforting to know you don't have to conform to peer pressure. God knows you and loves you just as you are.

NO MORE SECRETS

If your secret is that you have a hard time saying no to your friends, let's do some work in this area right now. Take a few minutes to answer the following questions, either here or in your private notebook.

Think of a time when you felt pressured by your friends and write down what happened.

_____

_____

Why did you feel pressured and how did you respond?

_____

_____

Name one person you've hung out with that later you realized you shouldn't have? _____

What happened and what did you do?

_____

_____

Why do you think it is important to not give in when we feel pressure from others?

_____

_____

SECRET STRENGTH

"LORD, guard me from the power of wicked people; protect me from cruel people who plan to trip me up."—PSALM 140:4

Sometimes I think sexual thoughts *(and sometimes I act on those thoughts).*

*e*very day hundreds of sexual images intrude upon our lives. They surround us. They are on television, in advertisements, movies, DVDs, magazines, the Internet, and of course music. And there are the real-life guys we find attractive. As Sarah learned, it can be difficult to remain pure, even with the best intentions.

THE SECRET

Sarah's Story

I dated a guy in high school I really liked. It was the summer of my sopho-more year. He was funny, sweet, and nice. He was a college student, and I was a high school student. Most of the things we did were with the church group or with others who were involved with the church. I had only dated a handful of people by the time I was 16, and I was relatively inexperienced when it came to dating.

I only dated this guy for a few months. We would hang out, and it was great. We didn't really talk all that much about our thoughts, feelings, beliefs, or goals for our lives.

When we were alone, we would cuddle and kiss. Sometimes he would talk about how sexy I was, and it would make me feel really sexy. He would talk about things we could do, and I'd find myself thinking about what it would be like to do those things with him. He said he'd just stroke my naked body, and it would feel good, and we wouldn't have sex. I found myself being physically attracted to him and thinking more and more about allowing him to touch me.

The few times when he did try to do something inappropriate, I could see how tempting it might be to give in, and how smooth and caring guys seem when they want you to respond to them in a sexual way. But I said no and he backed away.

I really cared for this guy and I wanted to please him, so it might seem natural for me to want to do the things he wanted me to do in order to satisfy him, please him, or make him like me more. But I didn't feel comfortable getting involved with him physically for a number of reasons. I knew what God expected of me and how he hoped I would respond in a situation like that. I also didn't really know the guy all that well, and didn't feel comfortable giving that much of myself away to him. I also had a fear of getting pregnant.

After the summer was over, he went back to college, and he broke up with me a week or two later. If I would have slept with him or gone too far physically, I know I would have had some serious regrets. I am so glad God gave me the wisdom and protection I needed in that situation.

UNLOCKING THE SECRET

As Sarah discovered, impure thoughts can tempt us to have sex before marriage. God created sex, and he intends for us to enjoy sex in its rightful place, within marriage. He knows what's best for us and what we can handle, which is why he set up boundaries or biblical guidelines for sex.

Sex within marriage allows us to become physically, emotionally, and spiritually connected with another person. It is part of the potential to be truly known by someone who has committed to us their lifetime partnership and a bond of safety. Outside of marriage, sex can create the wrong kind of intimacy. We can feel robbed if we give too much of ourselves away too soon, and to the wrong person(s). It can also harm us physically, emotionally, and spiritually.

We all have the desire to be loved and cared for, and sometimes the idea of sex makes us feel like we can fill that void. But sexual immorality (sex outside of its rightful context) is a sin. We can also avoid a lot of negative consequences by choosing to remain pure. When we give ourselves away physically outside of a committed, safe marriage, we experience a level of emotion and connectedness that is bigger than the foundation of dating can handle. Eventually, intensity and insecurity arise in not having the surety of a commitment before God.

Sexual feelings can be misleading. We can mistake sexual arousal for love when it is hormonally driven. That's why infatuation is so great, because with those hormones bubbling we feel so good—like a natural high. That's not to say that you can't really love someone whom you have sexual feelings toward, but love grows over time and it is rarely at first sight. Sarah made a good choice, and she stood up for what she believed in. But with all of the pressures and influences we have in our culture, having sex can be a temptation for many of us. It's not always easy to make the right choice. So what can you do?

- Dress modestly. How you dress reflects a message about you.
- Guard your mind. Avoid images that cause you to stumble or tempt you, or wishful thinking that is not based in what is real.
- Don't think that just because you love someone that it is okay to have sex before marriage.
- Decide how far is too far before you get into the situation.

- Avoid the fantasy that romance, love, and sex will make you special to the guy you are with or that it will be different with you.
- Know God has your best interest at heart in regard to sex and purity.

If you tend to think that more guys would like you if you dress and act sexy, the truth is you may be drawing the wrong kind of attention to yourself. Guys are motivated by what they see, and they are tempted sexually that way.

One thing you can do is set up physical boundaries that can help keep you from entering into the danger zone. Going too far includes sexual intercourse, oral sex, and "petting" (stimulating your boyfriend's sexual organs or having him stimulate yours).

You can also guard your heart and honor your body. First Corinthians 6:18–20 tells us to steer clear of sexual sin: "So run away from sexual sin. Every other sin people do is outside their bodies, but those who sin sexually sin against their own bodies. You should know that your body is a temple for the Holy Spirit who is in you. You have received the Holy Spirit from God. So you do not belong to yourselves, because you were bought by God for a price. So honor God with your bodies."

Some of you will get caught up in ideas of love and romance—thoughts and fantasies—that can lead you to sexual relating. What we allow our minds to daydream about affects what we do and feel. Therefore, for most women, emotional connection influenced by romantic fantasies can lead to sexual connection. And once you start down a path of being sexually stimulated, it becomes increasingly more enticing. If your body responds the way God intended it to, and it was a pleasurable experience, you're going to want more. First, you can thank God that your body works and then ask him to help you delay sexual gratification until it's biblically right.

Lies and Truth about Sex

- Lie: My boyfriend won't love me anymore if I don't have sex with him. (Truth: If he loves you, he'll wait.)
- Lie: We can have safe sex if we use a condom. (Truth: *No* form of birth control is 100 percent effective.)
- Lie: Oral sex is okay; it's not really sex. (Truth: It's sex. That's why it's called oral *sex*.)
- Lie: Nothing will happen if I only have sex once. (Truth: You can become pregnant or catch a social disease such as AIDS by just having sex one time. And you'll be tempted to have sex again.)
- Lie: I've already had sex once so it's okay to do it again. (Truth: Nope. You're taking chances with your physical, emotional, and spiritual well-being.)
- Lie: I can prove to the person I'm dating that I love him by having sex. (Truth: You never have to prove your love to someone who really cares for you.)

Sometimes you can find yourself in situations that make you wonder if you're normal or not. Maybe you're not much into "liking" guys and when the girls at school start going boy crazy, you're disinterested and would rather be with your horse or riding your skateboard. It may just be that this part of your emotional development hasn't gotten there yet. Or if you've experienced sexual, physical, or emotional abuse where your "trust meter" has been broken, then you may shy away from intimacy altogether. Or you may react in the opposite way by becoming hypersexual, giving your body away but not your heart because you feel like damaged goods.

What if your secret struggle is same-sex attraction? As I have said before, girls' best friends are strong bonds that are the pre-training to dating. While you can be excited about and always want to be with a new friend, these relationships are usually just friendships. But what if you start having sexual feelings for your best friend? Maybe you are curious because you've heard people joke about girls kissing girls or you've seen stuff on TV and the Internet. You may wonder if this means you are gay? You may have never thought of actually being physical with a girlfriend but can't stop thinking about the idea of it. Or you may have a friend who has tried to get you to do something sexual just to be different or explore sexual behaviors. Even if you have had a same-sex sexual experience, this does not automatically mean you are a lesbian. And this is especially true if drugs or alcohol were involved at the time of the encounter, or if you couldn't say no for fear of losing the friendship. Remember, as a young person it is not uncommon to try on a lot of different ways of being, like trying on different outfits to see what fits.

If you find yourself not sure about your sexual thoughts and feelings, ask yourself what you are truly longing for as the outcome. Also, ask yourself about how you feel about each of your parents. Do you spend time with them? Do you feel they understand you? And the bond you have with a same-sex attraction, does it seem balanced or over the top? Where does God fit into these feelings? And would this really be his best for you? Lots of things feel good—as if we can't live without them—but not all things we feel are good for us. Find out what your feelings mean instead of just giving into them. If you have difficulty keeping sexual boundaries then find someone whom you can talk to. Many churches have groups for people with same-sex attraction struggles.

When I was in high school, my youth pastor told us a story

that related to sexual purity that I've never forgotten. He said that we were all beautifully wrapped Christmas presents under God's tree, waiting for Christmas morning. But sometimes it is hard to wait, and we want to peek at those presents early. Sometimes we pull the paper back and try to get a glimpse of what's inside. Other times we may completely unwrap a gift, and then we feebly try to re-wrap it and put it back under the tree, hoping no one will notice. But on Christmas morning, the re-wrapped gifts are usually the ones we leave until last. And they don't seem so special, because we already know what is inside. This is what happens when we go too far sexually outside of marriage and allow ourselves or someone else to be unwrapped.

We can never re-wrap ourselves the way God can. But the good thing is that if we turn to him and confess our sins, he is in the re-wrapping business, and is the only one who can re-wrap us to our original beauty and specialness. If you have been unwrapped, turn to him. He can re-wrap you, and he will if you let him.

NO MORE SECRETS

If your secret is the impure thoughts in your head (or acting on those thoughts), let's do some work in this area right now. Answer the following questions, either here or in your private notebook.

What do you think "remaining pure" means?

_____

_____

_____

Why does God want us to save sex for marriage?

_____

_____

_____

How can you avoid impure thoughts, such as those triggered by sexually oriented music, movies, and pornography?

_____

_____

_____

SECRET STRENGTH

"They are blessed whose thoughts are pure, for they will see God."—MATTHEW 5:8

I was raped.

O ne of the secrets a lot of women keep, regardless of their age, is rape. But failing to talk to someone about what happened can cause other problems such as depression, suicidal thoughts, feelings of worthlessness, and fear.

THE SECRET

Elaina's Story

I grew up in a Christian home, and I have attended church all of my life. I realized later, in my heart I was not a true believer, rather I just did what was expected of me by my family and the church members.

During my sophomore year in high school, I was in a relationship with a guy I cared about and trusted. We'd been friends for a while. He was popular and everyone liked him. The truth is that sometimes I felt lucky he even talked to me.

One weekend we went to a place that's like a huge warehouse with the latest games. It had everything from video games to laser tag to those little race cars. And it had a food court in it. Some of our friends met us there. It's a very casual place. I went in jeans, a T-shirt, and a cute jacket. I pulled my hair back in a ponytail. I'd worn this on a church trip a few weeks before.

We had a great time. When the evening was over, he took me out for a ride to show me a place he'd found. He was driving his dad's SUV. He took me to an area that was very isolated, where we could see the stars, talk, cuddle a little, and kiss some. I'm ashamed to admit it, but we'd done this before—but all we'd ever done was kiss a little.

This time it was different. This time his hands were all over me, places they shouldn't have been. I kept telling him to stop, but then he penned me under him. I could barely move. He actually tore my T-shirt off of me. By that time I was screaming. He knew I was a virgin, but he didn't stop until he had forced himself inside me. He had raped me!

> I KEPT TELLING HIM TO STOP, BUT THEN HE PENNED ME UNDER HIM.

When it was over, I was crying and he said, "It'll be better next time."

I said, "I told you to stop."

And he started saying that it wasn't his fault, it was my fault. I was so sexy, and he knew I wanted to have sex—and he wanted my first time to be with him. That we'd dated for a while and a guy has needs. My whole body hurt, and I was so confused. I just wanted to go home. He helped me get my things together and get dressed and took me home. He walked me to the door, and then he tried to kiss me good night like nothing had happened—like I had been a willing participant.

I was so embarrassed. As soon as I got in the house, I locked the door and turned back on the alarm. Then I ran upstairs and took a shower. I scrubbed and scrubbed as if somehow that would make everything better.

I didn't tell my parents because I knew they'd be disappointed in me. I lied to my friends, and I never went out with him again. I spent almost all of the next month worried that I might be pregnant, but I was relieved to find out I wasn't. I continued to act like nothing had ever happened, but I was hurting badly on the inside. And I kept thinking, Maybe it was my fault. Maybe I lead him on like he said. Am I a tease?

Sometimes I think some of his friends knew, because of the way they worded things they said to me. I wasn't really sure what to do. I didn't want to date anyone and avoided going out in the same group of friends for fear he'd be there. My parents were noticing that I wasn't as happy and active as I had been.

I thought I could keep my secret and move on without any help, but I was sinking into a depression. I felt bad about myself; I didn't trust any guys my age; I no longer went to church; I stayed in my room a lot. I kept replaying that day and night in my head, wondering what I had done to make him attack me. Then one day thoughts of suicide started running through my head.

Every 2 minutes someone in the U.S. is sexually assaulted. Almost 2/3 of rapes were committed by someone known to the victim. In their lifetime 1 in 6 women and 1 in 33 men will be victims of sexual assault. 44% of all rape victims are under age 18, and 80% are under age 30.
—The Rape, Abuse and Incest National Network (www.rainn.org)

At the end of my junior year of high school, a girlfriend I'd known most of my life invited me to spend the night at her house. We'd had dozens of sleepovers, but this time it was exactly one year since the rape. I tried to keep my mind off of it, but I couldn't. I started crying, and finally I broke down and told her what happened. She was very quiet and just put her arm around me and kept saying things like: "It wasn't your fault." "You said no. When a girl says no, the guy is supposed to stop." "You're not a tease. He raped you." We talked for a long time, and she convinced me to start going to church again. I was hesitant, but the leaders reached out to me and made me feel comfortable. So many people were glad that I was back—especially my parents. That year at church camp I recommitted my life to God and surrendered completely to him.

My friend introduced me to a member of the church who was a psychologist. She had helped my friend work out some problems. I really liked this lady. And then my friend asked me if I would tell the psychologist or let her tell the psychologist what happened. I knew I was having more and more thoughts of suicide, so

I said yes. They arranged a time where we could talk privately, and it helped me a lot. Eventually I told my parents. I thought they would be disappointed and mad at me, but they weren't. They were very supportive. I went into counseling. My parents went into counseling, too, so they could help me through this.

Sometimes, when I'm on a date, I still struggle with the fear of being raped. I'm beginning to realize that rape is not about sex; it's really about controlling someone.

UNLOCKING THE SECRET

Almost two-thirds of rapes are committed by someone known to the victim, according to the Rape, Abuse and Incest National Network. And Elaina is right that rape is about control and not sex. Rape is an act of violence. And it is considered rape when anyone is *forced* into a sexual act.

The sad thing is that so many girls keep rape a secret, when telling would help the girls heal spiritually, physically, and emotionally. Why would a girl keep rape a secret? For the same reason girls have kept rape a secret for generations: They may wrongly feel embarrassed, ashamed, maybe even dirty. Sometimes the girl believes a rapist when he lies and says she led him on. Sometimes she can't let herself see the guy she's dated and trusted as a rapist. Sometimes it's because she doesn't want to admit she's been raped. Sometimes calling someone a rapist or accusing him of rape can sound so extreme when you know the person. Therefore most victims and friends will minimize the guy's actions. And after living through being raped, she may also fear being the one her friends "turn on" for accusing the popular guy of something so horrible.

When girls keep secrets like being raped, they tend to develop other problems. Elaina became depressed, stopped going out, and had suicidal thoughts. If she had shared her secret earlier, she might have avoided many of those problems.

> Among high school students surveyed nationwide, about 8% reported having been forced to have sex. Females (11%) were more likely to report having been forced to have sex than males (4%).
>
> —Centers for Disease Control and Prevention

Sometimes girls who are virgins don't feel pure after a rape. But rape is a crime. As much as the rapist might want you to believe he took away your virtue, in so many ways he did not—because you did not choose to have sex with him. To lose your virtue, you must have chosen to have sex. It is an emotional and physical choice you make. If you are raped, God sees this as sin against you, not you choosing to sin. God knows your pain and shame, and in this world we unfortunately have to work through the consequences of others sinning against us. God will still honor your choice to be sexually pure. Not all is ruined, and each day we can choose to put the past behind us. Out of ashes God can bring forth new life.

If you go through something as tough as Elaina went through, including physical abuse and rape, you are going to feel pain. But don't keep that pain to yourself. Tell others. Even if you were raped a long time ago, it will help you to tell someone you trust your secret. If the person you tell doesn't believe you, then go to the next person on your list. If you are uncomfortable telling your secret to someone you know, call or go online and contact via chat one of the many rape hotline centers and talk to someone. Some are listed in the Resources section that starts on page 217.

Elaina's struggle shows us how a Christian's life isn't always one of a straight and easy path. Each person experiences ups and downs. Even though there were times Elaina didn't feel his presence, God kept making himself known to her through people and his Word. God keeps pursuing us and never gives up on us, even when we give up on ourselves.

Like Elaina, there are times in my own life when I've needed God to bring me peace, and he's comforted me in ways that nothing or no one else could or can.

Living a Christian life doesn't mean that you will never experience any pain or that things won't happen to you that are out of your control. Yet God's love can bring you through a variety of hurtful or painful experiences. If you are hurting right now, there is help available to you. You might want to begin by praying to God and asking for his help. Talking to a friend, parent, or someone else will also help you to sort out the way you feel.

NO MORE SECRETS

Like Elaina, you, too, can surrender your hurt and allow God to help you. Remember, surrender is not a one-time event, but something we must do again and again to allow God to control our lives. If your secret is being raped, the following may help you let go of your hurt and pain:

- Seeking God
- Praying
- Loving yourself

- Talking to someone else about how you feel
- Forgiving others

- Accepting help from others
- Allowing God to heal your heart

Take a few minutes to answer the following questions, either here or in your private notebook.

I have experienced hurt or pain in my life when

_____

God has shown his love to me by

_____

_____

I will start letting go of the past and letting God help me by
(Check all that apply.)
- ○ Seeking him in all things
- ○ Allowing healing to take place
- ○ Forgiving others
- ○ Seeking professional help or guidance when necessary
- ○ Telling a friend or a parent what happened and how I feel

SECRET STRENGTH

"I asked the LORD for help, and he answered me. He saved me from all that I feared."—PSALM 34:4

Will the real me please stand up?

*d*o you ever feel like you are wearing a mask to hide your real feelings? And does the mask you wear depend on who you are with and where you are at that moment? Perhaps you're different at home than when you are in church or school. Maybe your parents see you as shy, but your friends say you're the life of the party! Maybe sometimes you hide your thoughts from everyone, because you feel no one understands you. Maybe sometimes you feel like a fraud. You are not alone! Depending on whom we are with and where we are, different people and situations bring out different aspects of our personality. But if your personality changes drastically from situation to situation, or if around certain people you feel confused about who you really are, you might need to work at discovering and being the authentic or true you.

THE SECRET

Taylor's Story

Sometimes I smile on the outside, but inside I'm having bad thoughts. I know God is not happy with me when I have such thoughts, but what do I do when I'm thinking things like hoping the coach is sick so we will have a sub-stitute for gym class and can just sit around and talk. Or when the homeroom teacher needed someone to help her, and I was one of the people she chose. I didn't want to help her, but I did anyway and I pretended to be happy. Or the other day my mom had something to do and she wanted me to take care of my little brothers. So instead of going shopping with my friends, I had to stay home. I was really mad. I took care of my brothers, but I just ordered them around. I didn't play with them. Just when I was wishing I was an only child, my five-year-old brother came and gave me a big hug. I almost cried. Are my selfish thoughts the real me?

Brooke's Story

I feel like a fraud. It's like I keep trying on personalities searching to find the one that fits me. But none of them do. I don't even know who the real me is. Sometimes I'm wild and crazy. Sometimes I'm quiet and shy. Sometimes, I'm ashamed to say, I really throw a temper tantrum. I get frustrated just try-ing to figure out who I am and how to be the person others want me to be—and still be who I want to be. I'm really a lot of different people mixed together. Sometimes I think the pressure is so high to figure out who I am that I'll just burst into a thousand pieces.

Gianna's Story

I know what I want to be . . . I want to be someone who encourages people, and does special things for people, who really listens, and is interested in what people are doing. I want to be that lady who is sincere, nice, genuine, and nur-turing to everyone; who sees everyone as her brother and sister; someone who overlooks much, forgives much, loves much, and is beautiful inside and out, naturally. And I try really hard to be that person, but I don't always succeed.

One time I wrote a really long list of all the personality traits I wish I had, and then I realized that sometimes they contradicted each other like "I want to be someone who is prudent with money and lavish with gifts." And I started laughing and crying at the same time. My dad came in and asked me what was going on. I told him, and he gave me a hug and said to just keep trying to do the right things and soon I'll be the person God wants me to be.

Five big truths that will help you live an amazing life . . .

1. You're a unique creation of God.
2. You have the power to do much, be much, and give much.
3. You can be an encourager of others.
4. No matter what you've been through, God loves you. You are valuable to him, and he will use all things for good.
5. You can lead a life of purpose and make a difference in the world.

UNLOCKING THE SECRET

Our basic personalities are formed by seven years of age. From seven to eleven we concentrate on mastering basic skills and abilities. And around age twelve, we gain the capacity for abstract thinking and are able to reflect on ourselves in a way we were unable to before. This introduces a whole new array of feelings to sort out. Adolescence is a journey of fine-tuning and reworking things in a greater variety of settings. It is the time to try on, explore, and practice different parts of ourselves and decide what fits or works for us. At the end of this time, we are ready to break away from our safe environment and go out alone into the bigger world.

But the journey doesn't end there. Developing our sense of self and becoming the person God wants us to be is a lifelong journey. And it's not easy. Look through the secrets in this book. There are a lot of things out there to cause us to slip up.

At first, not being the "real" you might not seem like a harmful secret, but it becomes a harmful secret if you feel that you must drastically alter your personality to please others or fit in. You'll know this because your actions will probably not feel right to you. Talking about this to someone you trust can be a big help.

Maybe your secret is that you're not sure how to become who God wants you to be. Don't worry. Everyone must go through a time of figuring out God's design for him- or herself and then maturing in it. None of us get the answers all at once. To figure out who you are, you must live and experience life, reflect on your past and present choices, and ask for feedback from people you trust. Having a "sense of self" means that you are connected to others *and* are a separate person with your own likes and dislikes, values, and opinions.

Sometimes who you wish you were is different from who you realize you are. You may want to be a singer who shares God through song on stage. But if you don't have a talent for singing, then that's not where you would shine. Instead, maybe the true you is expressing yourself as a songwriter. There are many different ways to express the values and desires of your heart. Look for the one that fits you.

A natural part of growing into adulthood is learning how to accept and love who you are and who you are not, and what you can and cannot change. A lot happens to young women emotionally and physically between the ages of ten and twenty. Maybe your body has changed or is still changing, and your emotions might sometimes seem like a wild roller-coaster ride. And then you have the pressures of the media, your peers, your family—and pressures you might place on yourself—and fears of what the future will bring.

But when you find yourself frustrated or annoyed by life, take a deep breath, calm down, and remember that by always trying to do the right thing and seeing what fits and what doesn't, you are continuing to grow into the unique person God created you to be. And by choosing right things, your life will begin to show love, joy, peace, patience, kindness, goodness, faithfulness, gentleness, and self-control (Galatians 5:22–23).

In this great journey of life, each day is about seeking the Lord's counsel and learning how to be real with yourself, God, and others. Each day is about writing your own story. And each day you get a new start to be the person God knows you can be. So, if you think you really messed up today, start again. Ask for help. Pray. Tomorrow can be better.

NO MORE SECRETS

If your secret is that you aren't sure how to become the person God intends you to be, then let's do some work in this area right now. Take a few minutes to answer the following questions, either here or in your private notebook.

My standards, values, and morals include

_____

_____

Three things I'd like to improve about myself are

_____

_____

My passion for life is

_____

My vision for the future is

_____

God can use me to shine his light by

_____

"Do your best to add these things to your lives: to your faith, add goodness; and to your goodness, add knowledge; and to your knowledge, add self-control; and to your self-control, add patience; and to your patience, add service for God; and to your service for God, add kindness for your brothers and sisters in Christ; and to this kindness, add love. If all these things are in you and are growing, they will help you to be useful and productive in your knowledge of our Lord Jesus Christ. But anyone who does not have these things cannot see clearly. He is blind and has forgotten that he was made clean from his past sins."—2 Peter 1:5–9

SECRET STRENGTH

"In the same way, you should be a light for other people. Live so that they will see the good things you do and will praise your Father in heaven."—MATTHEW 5:16

NO MORE SECRETS, SAY HELLO TO THE NEW YOU!

Keeping a harmful secret chips away at our happiness. Only by opening the secret up and sharing it appropriately—with self, God, and someone else—can we hope to live a life of opportunity and authenticity, a life in which we are the same on the outside as on the inside, the life God wants us to lead.

"Then you will call my name. You will come to me and pray to me, and I will listen to you."—*JEREMIAH 29:12*

I don't know why we always think we're alone in our pain, or that nobody else could understand our experience, but somehow we do. Pain and shame are isolating; they make us instinctively want to hide ourselves. But the more we can be real and let people in, the more we realize that others are a mess too. We can stop taking ourselves so seriously. We can let a little more of our secret out. And when we do, others often reflect on their own experience. They say, "Yeah, me too!" and not only is a connection formed, both people feel more real and authentic, validated, and less alone.

Remember the pattern that causes the stress in the first place?

- We mess up.
- We feel guilty about it.
- We form a secret.

Then the more we live in our guilt, the easier it is for the enemy to use our guilt to keep us feeling shameful, unworthy, and *not good enough*. We feel like we're living dark, lonely, and worthless lives. As long as we stay in the dark with our secrets, we allow the enemy to keep us mired in muck.

The following stories are what some of you said happened when you finally revealed your secret. Can you see God's hand?

"I worked at a camp last summer and had a great time, but when I came home, I was really exhausted. All my friends from camp lived about eight hours away. For a long time I was keeping a secret about feeling depressed. I'd go home after school, sit on my bed, and just write in my notebook about how I was feeling. I never wanted to do homework. I never wanted to phone my old friends. But then I started talking about it, first to a friend at school—one I never thought I'd make—then to the school counselor, then to my mom. She helped get me on a different sleep schedule, got me some vitamins, and let me drop out of AP English, which I didn't like anyway. I'm starting to feel better. I'm glad I didn't keep my secret."—Jada

"Six months ago, my dad was fired from his job. It was a big misun-

derstanding where the boss got mad at him for something he didn't do. I was really mad at my dad's boss, because I know him and he goes to our church. Since Dad didn't have a job, we had to really tighten things down in the family. Dad seemed pretty down for a long time. I was so mad, but I didn't feel like I could tell anyone.

82% of you said you are **_satisfied with what you've achieved_** in your lives so far.

"Then I sat down with my dad, and we started talking. He asked me how I was feeling about his job. I don't know why, but I just started crying. I cried and cried. Dad didn't say anything; he just sat there with me and lightly stroked my back. When I finally stopped crying, we talked it out. I think things are going to be better now. I don't feel so angry inside." —Avery

"I had oral sex with my boyfriend twice. I know you're not supposed to, but we did. I felt really confused inside. I didn't know what God thought of me. I wasn't sure if I even loved my boyfriend or if he loved me. I wanted to talk to someone, but I didn't know who I could talk to. I didn't know what people would think if they found out. I know I couldn't ever tell my parents something like that.

"One day I decided to talk to my youth pastor's wife about it. She's pretty cool. I thought she might be shocked or angry with me, but instead she just listened for a long time, then prayed with me, and gave me a hug. She helped me set some boundaries with my boyfriend to help keep us accountable. She encouraged me to talk to my parents and said she'd be there with me if I wanted someone else there. I haven't done that yet, but maybe I will some other time."—Kristen

Welcome to the new you!

Your secret doesn't define you. It's not *who you are*. Your identity is in Christ, and "those who are in Christ Jesus are not judged guilty" (Romans 8:1). So I want to finish by encouraging you above all else to keep your eyes on Jesus Christ. Get connected spiritually by reading Scripture, praying, getting together with others in a good youth group or spiritual gathering, and creating space to hear God speaking in your life.

> WE'RE NOT MEANT TO DEAL WITH PROBLEMS IN OUR LIVES ALONE.

Get connected in truth by seeking support from others. Face the fear of being vulnerable. Take the risk of opening up. Seek wise counsel if you need it—from your parents, a pastor, a counselor, or a friend. We're not meant to deal with problems in our lives alone. We're meant to do it with one another. It's why Christ came, to show us the way. He came to be with us, so that we wouldn't have to find the way all by ourselves. So make sure you are connecting emotionally.

My prayer for you is Romans 15:13: "I pray that the God who gives hope will fill you with much joy and peace while you trust in him. Then your hope will overflow by the power of the Holy Spirit."

The freedom that Christ gives not only frees you from the pressure of your secrets, but it gives you the power and the courage you need in order to live your life to the fullest.

One step at a time.

This is the sixth step to living a secret-free life. Write down your thoughts in the space provided here or in your private notebook.

When something happens the enemy wants me to keep secret, I will

_____

_____

I can live a secret-free life by

_____

_____

Even if you do not have a secret right now, work through the Action Plan on page 214.

My prayer is

_____

_____

_____

Amen.

When you have a harmful secret or problem, a personal action plan can help you start on your solution. You can fill out an action plan for each of your secrets.

Personal resources

God has placed people around you who are willing to help you. Spend some time thinking about the people you can turn to with your secret(s). First would be your parents, but if you feel like you can't talk to your parents, seek out a teacher, school counselor, youth minister, pastor, parent of a friend, another family member such as your aunt, uncle, grandma, or grandpa, or a family friend. An older person can offer advice and perspective that a younger person is typically not going to be able to offer.

Below or in your notebook, list adults whom you feel comfortable discussing your secret with or calling in an emergency. If that person is not available or cannot help you, go to the next person on your list.

The adults I trust the most right now are

_____

name   phone / cell

_____

name   phone / cell

Are you unsure of how to tell your secret to the person you trust? Try using one of the following phrases to help get you started.

_____ (insert person's name), I need you to listen to some things that are hard for me to say. So please wait for me to finish before you respond. Okay?

_____ (insert person's name), I just need to bounce some ideas off of you. Can you listen for a few minutes?"

_____ (insert person's name), I feel like talking to you, but I'm not sure what I want to talk about. Can we just talk a bit?

Other resources

There are national, regional, and local Christian associations, support groups, and counseling centers available to help you for free or at a very low cost. Some are listed in the Resources section that starts on page 217. Others may be found in your local area by looking in the phone book or on the Internet, or by asking a trusted adult or a reference librarian to help you locate a source. If the first resource you call cannot help you, go to the next resource on your list.

_____

name   phone / cell

_____

name   phone / cell

What do I say?

You might be nervous when you talk with a trusted adult or contact a resource. Write some notes you can refer to about what you want to say. Remember: You don't have to tell your whole story in exact order right up front. You do need to name the secret, so the other person knows what it is too. Then explain how that person could help you, and ask if they are willing and able to help you. If they are willing, then you can provide more details. Expect them to ask questions that will help them understand how they can best help you. If you choose someone you don't know as well, of course start by being sure that person knows your name and how you know him or her. For example, you could say:

Hi, my name is _____ and I'm a member of _____ (or I know you from _____ or my friend _____ gave me your name). I'm struggling with a problem and need some help. I was wondering if you had some time to talk to me?

    I'm having a problem with _____. Right now, I'm feeling _____ (really scared, worried, that I might be pregnant, etc.). Can you help me with _____ (a plan, talking through what I'm feeling, telling my parents, etc.) or help me find resources that can help me in this situation (right now, when I'm ready, etc.)?

Now write your own script that fits a situation you are in and other notes on what you want to remember to say.

_____

_____

> *"Do not worry about anything, but pray and ask God*
> *for everything you need, always giving thanks."*
> *—PHILIPPIANS 4:6*

*C*ongratulations! You've taken a big step in finding someone to help you unravel your secret(s). To use this section, look under the topic of your secret(s). You'll find some of these resources under more than one topic, because several of the associations work with multiple concerns. Also, numbers that begin with (800) or (866) are toll-free calls on a landline. Remember: URLs are subject to change. Once you've called or gone online to locate a resource, the resource might be able to provide you with more information, more resources, and local resources to help you overcome your secret. Ask the resource's staff. Call them; e-mail them; blog with them. They are all passionate about helping you live a secret-free life.

Abortion
C.A.R.E., Inc., www.care1.org, (231) 745-0500.
Christian Family Services, www.christianfamilyservices.org, (803) 548-6030, (800) 489-6030.
Christian Life Resources, www.christianliferesources.com, (414) 774-1331.
Healing Love Outreach Ministries, www.hlom.org, (918) 706-8083.
Heartbeat International, www.heartbeatinternational.org, (614) 885-7577.
His Mansion Ministries, www.hismansion.com, (603) 464-5555.
Last Days Ministries, www.lastdaysministries.org; ordering tracks: (800) 228-9536.
Life Issues Institute, www.lifeissues.org, (513) 729-3600.
Mercy Ministries, www.mercyministries.org, (615) 831-6987.
National Right to Life, www.nrlc.org, (202) 626-8800.
New Life Ministries, www.newlife.com, (800) NEW-LIFE.

Abuse (mental)
C.A.R.E., Inc., www.care1.org, (231) 745-0500.
Healing Love Outreach Ministries, www.hlom.org, (918) 706-8083.
His Mansion Ministries, www.hismansion.com, (603) 464-5555.
Hope for Healing, www.hopeforhealing.org, (800) 656-4673.
Life Hurts, God Heals (LHGH), www.simplyyouthministry.com, (866) 9-simply.
Making Waves, www.mwaves.org, (506) 474-1666.
Mercy Ministries, www.mercyministries.org, (615) 831-6987.
National Association for Christian Recovery, www.nacronline.com, (714) 529-6227.
National Domestic Violence Hotline, www.ndvh.org, (800) 799-SAFE (7233).

National Teen Dating Abuse Helpline, www.loveisrespect.org, (866) 331-9474.
National Youth Violence Prevention Resource Center, www.safeyouth.org; site has a list of
crisis hotlines.
New Life Ministries, www.newlife.com, (800) NEW-LIFE.
Restore Troubled Teens, www.restoretroubledteens.com, (505) 391-0574.

Abuse (physical)

C.A.R.E., Inc., www.care1.org, (231) 745-0500.
Celebrate Recovery, www.saddlebackfamily.com/home/carehelp/celebrate_recovery.asp,
(949) 609-8334.
Healing Love Outreach Ministries, www.hlom.org, (918) 706-8083.
His Mansion Ministries, www.hismansion.com, (603) 464-5555.
Hope for Healing, www.hopeforhealing.org, (800) 656-4673.
Life Hurts, God Heals (LHGH), www.simplyyouthministry.com, (866) 9-simply.
Making Waves, www.mwaves.org, (506) 474-1666.
Mercy Ministries, www.mercyministries.com, (615) 831-6987.
National Association for Christian Recovery, www.nacronline.com, (714) 529-6227.
National Council on Child Abuse and Family Violence, www.nccafv.org, (202) 429-6695.
(Also a resource for other hotlines on abuse, such as NDVH below.)
National Domestic Violence Hotline, www.ndvh.org, (800) 799-SAFE (7233).
National Teen Dating Abuse Helpline, www.loveisrespect.org, (866) 331-9474.
National Youth Violence Prevention Resource Center, www.safeyouth.org; site has a list of
crisis hotlines.
New Life Ministries, www.newlife.com, (800) NEW-LIFE.
Restore Troubled Teens, www.restoretroubledteens.com, (505) 391-0574.

Abuse (sexual)

C.A.R.E., Inc., www.care1.org, (231) 745-0500.
Healing Love Outreach Ministries, www.hlom.org, (918) 706-8083.
His Mansion Ministries, www.hismansion.com, (603) 464-5555.
Hope for Healing, www.hopeforhealing.org, (800) 656-4673.
Life Hurts, God Heals (LHGH), www.simplyyouthministry.com, (866) 9-simply.
Mercy Ministries, www.mercyministries.com, (615) 831-6987.
National Association for Christian Recovery, www.nacronline.com, (714) 529-6227.
National Domestic Violence Hotline, www.ndvh.org, (800) 799-7233.
National Teen Dating Abuse Helpline, www.loveisrespect.org, (866) 331-9474.
National Youth Violence Prevention Resource Center, www.safeyouth.org; site has a list of
crisis hotlines.
New Life Ministries, www.newlife.com, (800) NEW-LIFE.
Restore Troubled Teens, www.restoretroubledteens.com, (505) 391-0574.

Addiction

Addictions Victorious, www.addvicinc.org, (866) 412-5252.
Al-Anon/Alateen, www.al-anon.org, (888) 425-2666.
Alcoholics Anonymous, www.alcoholics-anonymous.org, (212) 870-3400.
Alcoholics for Christ, www.alcoholicsforchrist.com, (800) 441-7877.
C.A.R.E., Inc., www.care1.org, (231) 745-0500.
Celebrate Recovery, www.saddlebackfamily.com/home/carehelp/celebrate_recovery.asp,
(949) 609-8334.
Evangel House, www.evangelhouse.com, (800) 924-4012.
Grace Track for Christians, www.christian-drug-alcohol-treatment.com, (800) 781-6113.
Healing Love Outreach Ministries, www.hlom.org, (918) 706-8083.

His Mansion Ministries, www.hismansion.com, (603) 464-5555.
Life Hurts, God Heals (LHGH), www.simplyyouthministry.com, (866) 9-simply.
Mercy Ministries, www.mercyministries.org, (615) 831-6987.
National Association for Christian Recovery, www.nacronline.com, (714) 529-6227.
National Children's Coalition, www.child.net/drugalc.htm, (415) 671-6670.
National Clearinghouse for Alcohol and Drug Information, www.health.org, (800) 729-6686.
National Council on Alcohol and Drug Abuse, www.ncadd.org, (800) 622-2255.
National Council on Problem Gambling, www.ncpgambling.org, (800) 522-4700.
New Life Ministries, www.newlife.com, (800) NEW-LIFE.
Restore Troubled Teens, www.restoretroubledteens.com, (505) 391-0574.

Adoption

American Family Association, www.afa.net, (662) 844-5036.
Christian Family Services, www.christianfamilyservices.org, (803) 548-6030.
Christian Homes & Family Services, www.christianhomes.com, (800) 592-4725.
Christian Life Resources, www.christianliferesources.com, (414) 774-1331.
Healing Love Outreach Ministries, www.hlom.org, (918) 706-8083.
Heartbeat International, www.heartbeatinternational.org, (614) 885-7577.
Life Issues Institute, www.lifeissues.org, (513) 729-3600.
Mercy Ministries, www.mercyministries.org, (615) 831-6987.
National Right to Life, www.nrlc.org, (202) 626-8800.
New Life Ministries, www.newlife.com, (800) NEW-LIFE.

Alcohol

Addictions Victorious, www.addvicinc.org, (866) 412-5252.
Al-Anon/Alateen, www.al-anon.org, (888) 425-2666.
Alcoholics Anonymous, www.alcoholics-anonymous.org, (212) 870-3400.
Alcoholics for Christ, www.alcoholicsforchrist.com, (800) 441-7877.
C.A.R.E., Inc., www.care1.org, (231) 745-0500.
Celebrate Recovery, www.saddlebackfamily.com/home/carehelp/celebrate_recovery.asp, (949) 609-8334.
Evangel House, www.evangelhouse.com, (800) 924-4012.
Grace Track for Christians, www.christian-drug-alcohol-treatment.com, (800) 781-6113.
Healing Love Outreach Ministries, www.hlom.org, (918) 706-8083.
His Mansion Ministries, www.hismansion.com, (603) 464-5555.
Hope for Healing, www.hopeforhealing.org, (800) 656-4673.
Life Hurts, God Heals (LHGH), www.simplyyouthministry.com, (866) 9-simply.
Mercy Ministries, www.mercyministries.org, (615) 831-6987.
National Association for Christian Recovery, www.nacronline.com, (714) 529-6227.
National Children's Coalition, www.child.net/drugalc.htm, (415) 671-6670.
National Clearinghouse for Alcohol and Drug Information, www.health.org, (800) 729-6686.
National Council on Alcohol and Drug Abuse, www.ncadd.org, (800) 622-2255.
National Youth Violence Prevention Resource Center, www.safeyouth.org; site has a list of crisis hotlines.
New Life Ministries, www.newlife.com, (800) NEW-LIFE.
Restore Troubled Teens, www.restoretroubledteens.com, (505) 391-0574.
Teen Challenge, www.teenchallengemidwest.com, (785) 984-2360.

Anger

Evangel House, www.evangelhouse.com, (800) 924-4012.
His Mansion Ministries, www.hismansion.com, (603) 464-5555.
Life Hurts, God Heals (LHGH), www.simplyyouthministry.com, (866) 9-simply.

Mercy Ministries, www.mercyministries.org, (615) 831-6987.
National Crime Prevention Council, www.ncpc.org, (202) 466-6272.
National Teen Dating Abuse Helpline, www.loveisrespect.org, (866) 331-9474.
National Youth Violence Prevention Resource Center, www.safeyouth.org; site has a list of
　　crisis hotlines.
New Life Ministries, www.newlife.com, (800) NEW-LIFE.

Anxiety/Fear/Phobia

Evangel House, www.evangelhouse.com, (800) 924-4012.
His Mansion Ministries, www.hismansion.com, (603) 464-5555.
Life Hurts, God Heals (LHGH), www.simplyyouthministry.com, (866) 9-simply.
Mercy Ministries, www.mercyministries.org, (615) 831-6987.
New Life Ministries, www.newlife.com, (800) NEW-LIFE.

Bipolar/Schizophrenia

American Academy of Child Adolescent Psychiatry, www.aacap.org, (202) 966-7300.
Depression and Bipolar Support Alliance, www.dbsalliance.org, (800) 826-3632.
Evangel House, www.evangelhouse.com, (800) 924-4012.
Focus Adolescent Services, www.focusas.com, (410) 341-4216.
His Mansion Ministries, www.hismansion.com, (603) 464-5555.
Life Hurts, God Heals (LHGH), www.simplyyouthministry.com, (866) 9-simply.
Mercy Ministries, www.mercyministries.org, (615) 831-6987.
New Life Ministries, www.newlife.com, (800) NEW-LIFE.

Criminal Issues

Evangel House, www.evangelhouse.com, (800) 924-4012.
Julian Youth Academy, www.teenrescue.com, (800) 494-2200.
Mercy Ministries, www.mercyministries.org, (615) 831-6987.
National Crime Prevention Council, www.ncpc.org, (202) 466-6272.
National Teen Dating Abuse Helpline, www.loveisrespect.org, (866) 331-9474.
New Life Ministries, www.newlife.com, (800) NEW-LIFE.

Cutting

Addictions Victorious, www.addvicinc.org, (866) 412-5252.
American Academy of Child Adolescent Psychiatry, www.aacap.org, (202) 966-7300.
C.A.R.E., Inc., www.care1.org, (231) 745-0500.
Celebrate Recovery, www.saddlebackfamily.com/home/carehelp/celebrate_recovery.asp,
　　(949) 609-8334.
Evangel House, www.evangelhouse.com, (800) 924-4012.
His Mansion Ministries, www.hismansion.com, (603) 464-5555.
Hope for Healing, www.hopeforhealing.org, (800) 656-4673.
Life Hurts, God Heals (LHGH), www.simplyyouthministry.com, (866) 9-simply.
Mercy Ministries, www.mercyministries.org, (615) 831-6987.
National Association for Christian Recovery, www.nacronline.com, (714) 529-6227.
New Life Ministries, www.newlife.com, (800) NEW-LIFE.
Restore Troubled Teens, www.restoretroubledteens.com, (505) 391-0574.

Depression

American Academy of Child Adolescent Psychiatry, www.aacap.org, (202) 966-7300.
C.A.R.E., Inc., www.care1.org, (231) 745-0500.
Depression and Bipolar Support Alliance, www.dbsalliance.org, (800) 826-3632.
Evangel House, www.evangelhouse.com, (800) 924-4012.
Healing Love Outreach Ministries, www.hlom.org, (918) 706-8083.

His Mansion Ministries, www.hismansion.com, (603) 464-5555.
Hope for Healing, www.hopeforhealing.org, (800) 656-4673.
Life Hurts, God Heals (LHGH), www.simplyyouthministry.com, (866) 9-simply.
Mercy Ministries, www.mercyministries.org, (615) 831-6987.
National Association for Christian Recovery, www.nacronline.com, (714) 529-6227.
New Life Ministries, www.newlife.com, (800) NEW-LIFE.
Restore Troubled Teens, www.restoretroubledteens.com, (505) 391-0574.

Disabilities

Christian Horizons, www.christian-horizons.org, (616) 956-7063.
Echoing Hills Village, www.echoinghillsvillage.org, (800) 419-6513.
Joni and Friends Ministry, www.joniandfriends.org, (800) 523-5777.
New Life Ministries, www.newlife.com, (800) NEW-LIFE.

Divorce

Life Hurts, God Heals (LHGH), www.simplyyouthministry.com, (866) 9-simply.
New Life Ministries, www.newlife.com, (800) NEW-LIFE.

Drug Abuse

Addictions Victorious, www.addvicinc.org, (866) 412-5252.
Al-Anon/Alateen, www.al-anon.org, (888) 425-2666.
Alcoholics Anonymous, www.alcoholics-anonymous.org, (212) 870-3400.
Alcoholics for Christ, www.alcoholicsforchrist.com, (800) 441-7877.
C.A.R.E., Inc., www.care1.org, (231) 745-0500.
Celebrate Recovery, www.saddlebackfamily.com/home/carehelp/celebrate_recovery.asp,
    (949) 609-8334.
Evangel House, www.evangelhouse.com, (800) 924-4012.
Grace Track for Christians, www.christian-drug-alcohol-treatment.com, (800) 781-6113.
Healing Love Outreach Ministries, www.hlom.org, (918) 706-8083.
His Mansion Ministries, www.hismansion.com, (603) 464-5555.
Hope for Healing, www.hopeforhealing.org, (800) 656-4673.
Life Hurts, God Heals (LHGH), www.simplyyouthministry.com, (866) 9-simply.
Mercy Ministries, www.mercyministries.org, (615) 831-6987.
National Association for Christian Recovery, www.nacronline.com, (714) 529-6227.
National Children's Coalition, www.child.net/drugalc.htm, (415) 671-6670.
National Clearinghouse for Alcohol and Drug Information, www.health.org, (800) 729-6686.
National Council on Alcohol and Drug Abuse, www.ncadd.org, (800) 622-2255.
National Youth Violence Prevention Resource Center, www.safeyouth.org; site has a list of
    crisis hotlines.
New Life Ministries, www.newlife.com, (800) NEW-LIFE.
Restore Troubled Teens, www.restoretroubledteens.com, (505) 391-0574.
Teen Challenge, www.teenchallengemidwest.com, (785) 984-2360.

Eating Disorders

Addictions Victorious, www.addvicinc.org, (866) 412-5252.
Anorexia Nervosa and Related Eating Disorders, Inc. (ANRED), www.anred.com. (See also
    National Association of Anorexia Nervosa and Associated Disorders, www.anad.org.)
C.A.R.E., Inc., www.care1.org, (231) 745-0500.
Celebrate Recovery, www.saddlebackfamily.com/home/carehelp/celebrate_recovery.asp,
    (949) 609-8334.
Eating Disorder Recovery Center, www.addictions.net, (866) 706-7111.
Evangel House, www.evangelhouse.com, (800) 924-4012.

Healing Love Outreach Ministries, www.hlom.org, (918) 706-8083.
His Mansion Ministries, www.hismansion.com, (603) 464-5555.
Life Hurts, God Heals (LHGH), www.simplyyouthministry.com, (866) 9-simply.
Mercy Ministries, www.mercyministries.org, (615) 831-6987.
National Association of Anorexia Nervosa and Associated Disorders, www.anad.org,
　　(847) 831-3438.
New Life Ministries, www.newlife.com, (800) NEW-LIFE.
Overeaters Anonymous, www.oa.org, (505) 891-2664.
Remuda Ranch, www.remudaranch.com, (800) 445-1900.
Restore Troubled Teens, www.restoretroubledteens.com, (505) 391-0574.

Faith
New Life Ministries, www.newlife.com, (800) NEW-LIFE.
Passion Conferences, www.268generation.com, (678) 366-9192.
Teen Mania, www.teenmania.org, (800) 299-TEEN / (800) 299-8336.
The Revolve Tour, www.revolvetour.com, (877) 9-REVOLVE.
Women of Faith Conferences, www.womenoffaith.com, (888) 49-FAITH / (888) 493-2484.

Family Problems
C.A.R.E., Inc., www.care1.org, (231) 745-0500.
Celebrate Recovery, www.saddlebackfamily.com/home/carehelp/celebrate_recovery.asp,
　　(949) 609-8334.
Diamond Ranch Academy, www.diamondranchacademy.com, (877) 372-3200.
Evangel House, www.evangelhouse.com, (800) 924-4012.
Focus on the Family, www.family.org, (800) 232-6459.
Mercy Ministries, www.mercyministries.org, (615) 831-6987.
National Association for Christian Recovery, www.nacronline.com, (714) 529-6227.
National Domestic Violence Hotline, www.ndvh.org, (800) 799-SAFE (7233).
National Teen Dating Abuse Helpline, www.loveisrespect.org, (866) 331-9474.
National Youth Violence Prevention Resource Center, www.safeyouth.org; site has a list of
　　crisis hotlines.
New Life Ministries, www.newlife.com, (800) NEW-LIFE.
Restore Troubled Teens, www.restoretroubledteens.com, (505) 391-0574.

Fear
Mercy Ministries, www.mercyministries.org, (615) 831-6987.
National Teen Dating Abuse Helpline, www.loveisrespect.org, (866) 331-9474
National Youth Violence Prevention Resource Center, www.safeyouth.org; site has a list of
　　crisis hotlines.
New Life Ministries, www.newlife.com, (800) NEW-LIFE.

Finances (debt and spending habits)
Crown Financial Ministries, www.crown.org, (770) 534-1000.
Dave Ramsey, www.daveramsey.com, (615) 371-8881, or on air (888) TALK-BAK.
New Life Ministries, www.newlife.com, (800) NEW-LIFE.

Fitness and Exercise
Mercy Ministries, www.mercyministries.org, (615) 831-6987.
New Life Ministries, www.newlife.com, (800) NEW-LIFE.
YWCA, www.ymca.net, (800) 872-9622.

Grief/Loss
American Academy of Child Adolescent Psychiatry, www.aacap.org, (202) 966-7300.

C.A.R.E., Inc., www.care1.org, (231) 745-0500.
Compassionate Friends, www.compassionatefriends.com, (630) 990-0010.
Grief Recovery Institute, www.grief-recovery.com, (818) 907-9600.
Grief Share, www.griefshare.org, (800) 395-5755.
His Mansion Ministries, www.hismansion.com, (603) 464-5555.
Mercy Ministries, www.mercyministries.org, (615) 831-6987.
National Association for Christian Recovery, www.nacronline.com, (714) 529-6227.
New Life Ministries, www.newlife.com, (800) NEW-LIFE.
Restore Troubled Teens, www.restoretroubledteens.com, (505) 391-0574.

Homosexuality

Addictions Victorious, www.addvicinc.org, (866) 412-5252.
Cross Ministry, www.crossministry.org, (919) 569-0375.
Exodus International, www.exodus-international.org, (888) 264-0877.
Healing Love Outreach Ministries, www.hlom.org, (918) 706-8083.
His Mansion Ministries, www.hismansion.com, (603) 464-5555.
Mercy Ministries, www.mercyministries.org, (615) 831-6987.
New Life Ministries, www.newlife.com, (800) NEW-LIFE.

Illness

New Life Ministries, www.newlife.com, (800) NEW-LIFE.

Incest

C.A.R.E., Inc., www.care1.org, (231) 745-0500.
Evangel House, www.evangelhouse.com, (800) 924-4012.
Healing Love Outreach Ministries, www.hlom.org, (918) 706-8083.
His Mansion Ministries, www.hismansion.com, (603) 464-5555.
Hope for Healing, www.hopeforhealing.org, (800) 656-4673.
Life Hurts, God Heals (LHGH), www.simplyyouthministry.com, (866) 9-simply.
Mercy Ministries, www.mercyministries.org, (615) 831-6987.
New Life Ministries, www.newlife.com, (800) NEW-LIFE.
Restore Troubled Teens, www.restoretroubledteens.com, (505) 391-0574.

Internet/Porn/Cybersex Addictions

Addictions Victorious, www.addvicinc.org, (866) 412-5252.
C.A.R.E., Inc., www.care1.org, (231) 745-0500.
Celebrate Recovery, www.saddlebackfamily.com/home/carehelp/celebrate_recovery.asp,
      (949) 609-8334.
Evangel House, www.evangelhouse.com, (800) 924-4012.
Healing Love Outreach Ministries, www.hlom.org, (918) 706-8083.
His Mansion Ministries, www.hismansion.com, (603) 464-5555.
Mercy Ministries, www.mercyministries.org, (615) 831-6987.
New Life Ministries, www.newlife.com, (800) NEW-LIFE.
Restore Troubled Teens, www.restoretroubledteens.com, (505) 391-0574.

Mental Health

American Academy of Child Adolescent Psychiatry, www.aacap.org, (202) 966-7300.
His Mansion Ministries, www.hismansion.com, (603) 464-5555.
Mercy Ministries, www.mercyministries.org, (615) 831-6987.
National Association for Christian Recovery, www.nacronline.com, (714) 529-6227.
New Life Ministries, www.newlife.com, (800) NEW-LIFE.
Restore Troubled Teens, www.restoretroubledteens.com, (505) 391-0574.

Music and Media

Al Menconi Ministries, www.Almenconi.com, (760) 591-4696.
Gospel Music Association (GMA), www.gospelmusic.org, (615) 242-0303.
New Life Ministries, www.newlife.com, (800) NEW-LIFE.
Plugged In, www.pluggedinonline.com (a Focus on the Family Web site), (800) 232-6459.
Women in Christian Media, www.womeninchristianmedia.org, (214) 319-7700.

Pornography

Addictions Victorious, www.addvicinc.org, (866) 412-5252.
Celebrate Recovery, www.saddlebackfamily.com/home/carehelp/celebrate_recovery.asp, (949) 609-8334.
Evangel House, www.evangelhouse.com, (800) 924-4012.
Healing Love Outreach Ministries, www.hlom.org, (918) 706-8083.
His Mansion Ministries, www.hismansion.com, (603) 464-5555.
Life Hurts, God Heals (LHGH), www.simplyyouthministry.com, (866) 9-simply.
Mercy Ministries, www.mercyministries.org, (615) 831-6987.
New Life Ministries, www.newlife.com, (800) NEW-LIFE.

Pregnancy

American Family Association, www.afa.net, (662) 844-5036.
Birthright International, www.Birthright.com, (800) 550-4900.
His Mansion Ministries, www.hismansion.com, (603) 464-5555.
Mercy Ministries, www.mercyministries.org, (615) 831-6987.
National Campaign to Prevent Teen and Unplanned Pregnancy, www.teenpregnancy.org, (202) 478-8500.
New Life Ministries, www.newlife.com, (800) NEW-LIFE.

Rape

C.A.R.E., Inc., www.care1.org, (231) 745-0500.
Healing Love Outreach Ministries, www.hlom.org, (918) 706-8083.
His Mansion Ministries, www.hismansion.com, (603) 464-5555.
Hope for Healing, www.hopeforhealing.org, (800) 656-4673.
Mercy Ministries, www.mercyministries.org, (615) 831-6987.
National Association for Christian Recovery, www.nacronline.com, (714) 529-6227.
National Teen Dating Abuse Helpline, www.loveisrespect.org, (866) 331-9474.
National Youth Violence Prevention Resource Center, www.safeyouth.org; site has a list of crisis hotlines.
New Life Ministries, www.newlife.com, (800) NEW-LIFE.
RAINN, www.rainn.org, (800) 656-HOPE.
Restore Troubled Teens, www.restoretroubledteens.com, (505) 391-0574.

Self-Esteem

C.A.R.E., Inc., www.care1.org, (231) 745-0500.
Evangel House, www.evangelhouse.com, (800) 924-4012.
Life Hurts, God Heals (LHGH), www.simplyyouthministry.com, (866) 9-simply.
Mercy Ministries, www.mercyministries.org, (615) 831-6987.
New Life Ministries, www.newlife.com, (800) NEW-LIFE.
Restore Troubled Teens, www.restoretroubledteens.com, (505) 391-0574.

Self-Injury/Self-Injury Awareness

C.A.R.E., Inc., www.care1.org, (231) 745-0500.
Evangel House, www.evangelhouse.com, (800) 924-4012.

Focus Adolescent Services, www.focusas.com/SelfInjury.html, (410) 341-4216.
Hope for Healing, www.hopeforhealing.org, (800) 656-4673.
Mercy Ministries, www.mercyministries.org, (615) 831-6987.
National Association for Christian Recovery, www.nacronline.com, (714) 529-6227.
National Youth Violence Prevention Resource Center, www.safeyouth.org; site has a list of
    crisis hotlines.
New Life Ministries, www.newlife.com, (800) NEW-LIFE.
Restore Troubled Teens, www.restoretroubledteens.com, (505) 391-0574.
Safe Alternatives, www.selfinjury.com, (800) DONTCUT / (800) 366-8288.

Sex Addiction
Addictions Victorious, www.addvicinc.org, (866) 412-5252.
C.A.R.E., Inc., www.care1.org, (231) 745-0500.
Evangel House, www.evangelhouse.com, (800) 924-4012.
Healing Love Outreach Ministries, www.hlom.org, (918) 706-8083.
His Mansion Ministries, www.hismansion.com, (603) 464-5555.
Mercy Ministries, www.mercyministries.org, (615) 831-6987.
National Association for Christian Recovery, www.nacronline.com, (714) 529-6227.
New Life Ministries, www.newlife.com, (800) NEW-LIFE.
Restore Troubled Teens, www.restoretroubledteens.com, (505) 391-0574.

Smoking
Addictions Victorious, www.addvicinc.org, (866) 412-5252.
C.A.R.E., Inc., www.care1.org, (231) 745-0500.
Celebrate Recovery, www.saddlebackfamily.com/home/carehelp/celebrate_recovery.asp,
    (949) 609-8334.
Evangel House, www.evangelhouse.com, (800) 924-4012.
Grace Track for Christians, www.christian-drug-alcohol-treatment.com, (800) 781-6113.
His Mansion Ministries, www.hismansion.com, (603) 464-5555.
Mercy Ministries, www.mercyministries.org, (615) 831-6987.
National Association for Christian Recovery, www.nacronline.com, (714) 529-6227.
National Children's Coalition, www.child.net/drugalc.htm, (415) 671-6670.
National Council on Alcohol and Drug Abuse, www.ncadd.org, (800) 622-2255.
New Life Ministries, www.newlife.com, (800) NEW-LIFE.
Restore Troubled Teens, www.restoretroubledteens.com, (505) 391-0574.

Spiritual Growth
Change Your Life Daily, www.beckytirabassi.com, (800) 444-6189.
Mercy Ministries, www.mercyministries.org, (615) 831-6987.
New Life Ministries, www.newlife.com, (800) NEW-LIFE.
Restore Troubled Teens, www.restoretroubledteens.com, (505) 391-0574.

Suicide
C.A.R.E., Inc., www.care1.org, (231) 745-0500.
Evangel House, www.evangelhouse.com, (800) 924-4012.
His Mansion Ministries, www.hismansion.com, (603) 464-5555.
Mercy Ministries, www.mercyministries.org, (615) 831-6987.
National Association for Christian Recovery, www.nacronline.com, (714) 529-6227.
National Youth Violence Prevention Resource Center, www.safeyouth.org; site has a list of
    crisis hotlines.
New Life Ministries, www.newlife.com, (800) NEW-LIFE.
Restore Troubled Teens, www.restoretroubledteens.com, (505) 391-0574.

Trauma

C.A.R.E., Inc., www.care1.org, (231) 745-0500.
Evangel House, www.evangelhouse.com, (800) 924-4012.
Healing Love Outreach Ministries, www.hlom.org, (918) 706-8083.
His Mansion Ministries, www.hismansion.com, (603) 464-5555.
National Association for Christian Recovery, www.nacronline.com, (714) 529-6227.
National Teen Dating Abuse Helpline, www.loveisrespect.org, (866) 331-9474.
National Youth Violence Prevention Resource Center, www.safeyouth.org; site has a list of crisis hotlines.
New Life Ministries, www.newlife.com, (800) NEW-LIFE.

Violence

C.A.R.E., Inc., www.care1.org, (231) 745-0500.
Evangel House, www.evangelhouse.com, (800) 924-4012.
His Mansion Ministries, www.hismansion.com, (603) 464-5555.
Hope for Healing, www.hopeforhealing.org, (800) 656-4673.
Making Waves, www.mwaves.org, (506) 474-1666.
National Association for Christian Recovery, www.nacronline.com, (714) 529-6227.
National Council on Child Abuse and Family Violence, www.nccafv.org, (202) 429-6695.
(Also a resource for other hotlines on abuse, such as NDVH below.)
National Domestic Violence Hotline, www.ndvh.org, (800) 799-SAFE (7233).
National Teen Dating Abuse Helpline, www.loveisrespect.org, (866) 331-9474.
National Youth Violence Prevention Resource Center, www.safeyouth.org. site has a list of crisis hotlines.
New Life Ministries, www.newlife.com, (800) NEW-LIFE.
Restore Troubled Teens, www.restoretroubledteens.com, (505) 391-0574.

Youth/Mentoring Programs

Diamond Ranch Academy, www.diamondranchacademy.com, (877) 372-3200.
Evangel House, www.evangelhouse.com, (800) 924-4012.
His Mansion Ministries, www.hismansion.com, (603) 464-5555.
Mercy Ministries, www.mercyministries.org, (615) 831-6987.
National Association for Christian Recovery, www.nacronline.com, (714) 529-6227.
National Children's Coalition, www.child.net/drugalc.htm, (415) 671-6670.
New Life Ministries, www.newlife.com, (800) NEW-LIFE.
Restore Troubled Teens, www.restoretroubledteens.com, (505) 391-0574.
YWCA, www.ymca.net, (800) 872-9622.